OUR LIFE in CHRIST®

High School
Bible Studies

Book 2

CPH®
Concordia Publishing House

Authors

Kurt Bickel, Tom Couser, Christopher Drager, Bianca Elliott, Jim Elsner, Mark Etter, Gretchen Gebhardt, Barrie Henke, James Klawiter, Reynold Kremer, Beth Orstadt, Craig Parrott, Jay Reed, Nikki Rochester, Ron Roma, Greg Rommel, Matthew Schaefer, Barney Schroeder, Ted Schroeder, Roger Sonnenberg, Susan Voss, Cynthia Werner

Editors

Tom Nummela
Mark Sengele

Your comments and suggestions concerning the material are appreciated. Please write the Editor of Youth Materials, Concordia Publishing House, 3558 S. Jefferson Avenue, St. Louis, MO 63118-3968.

This publication is also available in braille and in large type for the visually impaired. Call 1-800-433-3954 or write to Library for the Blind, 1333 S. Kirkwood Rd., St. Louis, MO 63122-7295.

Contents

*Our Life in Christ users please see the lesson reference chart
in the back of the book.*

Introduction

Our Life in Christ

We all need help to live our lives in Christ. The Bible is clear that sin afflicts the lives of all people, those who already believe in Christ and those who do not. The new life that Christ won for us through His suffering and death is created in us only by the power of the Holy Spirit working through the Gospel.

High school students are no exception. Their lives are often conflicted and torn as the result of sin. Sometimes it is sin from within, expressing itself in actions and attitudes that run counter to God's Law. Sometimes it is sin from other sources—the actions and attitudes of others—that disrupts their lives. They need help to live their lives in the joy and fullness that Christ desires.

Since it is the Gospel that brings life in Christ to people, it is our goal in these Bible studies for high school students to apply the Gospel to their life situations. These studies were prepared with four goals in mind. The lessons reflect these goals in the following ways:

- Each lesson presents the Gospel in ways that will help young people grow in their relationship with Christ.

- Each lesson is simple and direct—one page of instructions and helps for the Bible study leader and one reproducible page for the students to follow.

- Each study is practical and easy to prepare. Interaction, variety, and active learning are stressed without requiring excessive preparation by the Bible study leader.

- Each study deals with issues and topics that truly touch the lives of young people as they seek to live "in Christ."

This books contains 39 studies. They can be selected according to the needs of the students and leader and taught in any order. Note, however, that the first 14 studies are based on early Old Testament texts, beginning with creation and continuing through Esther. (Books 1 and 3 in this series use texts from later sections of the Old Testament.) The remaining studies focus on the life of Christ and the early Christian church. In each study, the Bible story is a means for considering a significant life issue for young people.

Helps for Preparation and Teaching

For ease of use, the leader page and student page for each study are printed side by side in this book, leader's material on the left and the corresponding student page on the right. The appropriate student page should be copied in a quantity sufficient for the class and distributed at the time indicated in the leader's notes.

It is assumed that the Bible class leader will have the usual basic classroom equipment and supplies available—pencils or pens for each student, blank paper (and occasionally tape or marking pens), and a chalkboard or its equivalent (white board, overhead transparency projector, or newsprint pad and easel) with corresponding markers or chalk. Encourage the students to bring their own Bibles. Then they can mark useful passages and make personal notes to guide their Bible study between classes. Do provide additional Bibles, however, for visitors or students who do not bring one.

The studies are outlined completely in the leader's notes, including a suggested time for each section of the study. The suggested times will total approximately 50–55 minutes, the maximum amount most Sunday morning Bible classes have available. Each session begins with an opening activity that may or may not be indicated on the student page. Teachers who regularly begin with prayer should include it before the opening activity. Most other parts of the study except the closing prayer are on both the leader page and student page and are indicated with corresponding numbers.

An average class size of 10 students is assumed. To facilitate discussion, especially when your class is larger than average, it is recommended to conduct much of the discussion in smaller groups—pairs, triads, or groups of five or six. Instructions to that effect are often included in the guide. If your class is small, you are already a "small group" and can ignore any such suggestions. Leaders who prefer to do all discussion with the class as a whole are also free to ignore small-group suggestions.

Most of the studies include one or two "Extending the Lesson" suggestions. Use these when the study progresses more quickly than expected, when your normal session exceeds 50–55 minutes, or when a suggested activity doesn't work with your group. They can also be used as "during the week" activities.

Of course, the leader is encouraged to review the study thoroughly well in advance of its presentation. Then the materials can be tailored to your individual students' needs and preferences as well as your own.

For Users of Our Life in Christ Sunday School Materials

One of the benefits of this book is to provide an opportunity for congregations using Our Life in Christ Sunday school materials to include their high school Bible classes in a "unified" curriculum. The studies in this book are based at least in part on the Bible story texts for the OLIC curriculum. High school students can study the same basic material as children in Sunday school classes and adults who use Our Life in Christ Adult Bible Studies. This can have great benefits for families as they discuss together what they are learning from God's Word.

A reference date on the leader page indicates the date on which that material is taught in the Our Life in Christ materials. In addition, a chart is printed in the back of the book showing the Our Life in Christ lesson numbers, titles, and Bible references.

1 God Does Good Work

Genesis 1:1–2:3 (OLIC: September 3, 2000)

Purpose

Students will explore the wonders of creation and celebrate what God has made as well as His continued care for His creation.

Opening (2 minutes). Invite the students to pray with you an ancient prayer in the words of Psalm 145:13–16.

1. Discovery Zone (15 minutes). Distribute copies of the student page and challenge students to consider what they know about the universe God created by thinking about microscopic discoveries and discoveries in space. Invite the students to work together in small groups of three to five to generate the two lists on the student page. You may have to give them some examples to get started—DNA or bacteria; galaxies or black holes. After groups have worked for about five minutes, ask each group to share its list. Remind students that these discoveries were made within the last 400 years—after the creation of the telescope and the microscope in the 17th century. Ask, "How were the people who lived before these discoveries different from you? How is God different before and after these discoveries?" (People's knowledge and lives were changed dramatically by scientific discovery. God, however, is unchanging—constant in His love for us.)

2. Into the Word (15 minutes). Invite the students to open their Bibles to Genesis 1. Tell them this is the account of the creation of the entire universe summed up in 31 verses. Ask different students to read each of the days of creation.

Instruct the students to turn to section 2 and discuss and respond to each of the selected passages. Some students will not be able to resist questions about life on other planets and the real age of the earth. Allow them to ask the questions without engaging in a debate. You can summarize the discus-

sion in the following manner:

"I don't think we have discovered everything there is to know about the universe. And some of the discoveries of the past seem to contradict each other (like Newtonian physics and quantum physics). One thing has not changed over the centuries—the account of Genesis. The first verse of the Bible is all encompassing. It is able to give an account of the magnificent and complex creation with simple and even poetic terms. Genesis 1–2 is inclusive of all the scientific discoveries ever made and yet to be made. All of it is good because God made it."

3. Scientific Discovery and God's Good Work (5 minutes). Instruct the students to look at the quotes in section 3 of the student page. Discuss the changing view of the universe in the last few centuries. Despite all the changes in how we see the world, God's view of us has not changed. Nothing is so small (microscopic) or so large (telescopic) that it escaped the creative, protective hand of God. How much more amazing, then, that He puts you and me—our physical and spiritual well-being—above everything else He has created! Heaven and earth will pass away, but because He sent His Son Jesus, we can spend eternity with Him. Ask the students to write in the space provided on the handout how they would like to be quoted regarding their view of the universe.

Closing (3 minutes). Close the session by listening to the students' quotes on the universe. Read Psalm 121.

Extending the Lesson

• Talk about God's continuing care for His creation. You may want to review this section from Luther's Small Catechism (questions 108–11).

God Does Good Work

Discovery Zone

List discoveries you have heard about that are in the microscopic world and discoveries you have heard about that are in outer space.

Things Too Small to See

Things Far-Off

Into the Word

How does the biblical account of the creation include the discoveries listed in section 1?

- Genesis 1:1

- Genesis 1:31

- Genesis 2:1

Scientific Discovery and God's Good Work

For centuries scientists viewed the universe according to Newtonian physics.

The universe is like a giant machine set in a framework of absolute time and space. Complicated movement can be understood as simple movement of the machine's inner parts, even if these parts can't be visualized. (The view of Sir Isaac Newton, 18th century)

With the discovery of quantum physics, scientists reach for new metaphors.

The universe begins to look more like a great thought than like a great machine. (James Jeans, 1930)

[The universe is] a vast porridge of being where nothing is fixed or measurable … somewhat ghostly and just beyond our grasp. (Danah Zohar, 1990)

Here is a quote that has endured over many, many centuries.

In the beginning God created the heavens and the earth. … God saw all that He had made, and it was very good. (Genesis 1:1, 31)

How would you want to be quoted regarding *your* view of the universe?

2 A Precious Gift

Genesis 2:4–25 (OLIC: September 10, 2000)

Purpose

God is the giver of all good things. Sexuality and relationships are among God's gifts—intended for our good, spoiled by sin, redeemed through Christ, and a model of His love for His people.

Opening (10 minutes). Prior to class make two signs: on one write "Disposable," on the other write "Irreplaceable." Post the two signs on opposite sides of the classroom. Ask the students to move to either side of the room depending on how they view each of the items. Begin by mentioning items that are obviously disposable (such as paper diapers or alkaline batteries). Move to things that are irreplaceable (famous art or an engagement ring). Include interpersonal relationships (your best friend or your first date). Ask the students to place the marriage relationship somewhere on the continuum. Discuss with students that society often views things as disposable. That makes life convenient, but it can become detrimental when that attitude extends to relationships, especially marriage.

1. For Adam and Eve (15 minutes). Distribute copies of the student page. If your class is large, divide into small groups. Direct the students to Genesis 2:4–25. Ask each group to consider the questions found on the worksheet. Ask each group to appoint one leader who is to help the group reach a common response to the questions. When you sense that all groups are finished, ask the groups to share their responses. Remind the students that God's purpose in uniting Adam and Eve was to provide companionship. His desire for Adam and Eve was a "one flesh," monogamous relationship of mutual respect and care—marriage.

2. For Us (10 minutes). Based on previous discussion, ask what God's desire is for teenagers when it comes to their sexuality. Allow the students to talk about the issue openly. Remind them that God's desire is that sexual intercourse is to be reserved for the marriage relationship. Direct the students to John 8:1–11, and ask a volunteer to read the passage aloud. Ask the participants to again discuss the questions on the student page in their small groups. God desires that all people honor the marriage relationship. He also stands ready to forgive all people, even those who commit the sin of adultery.

3. God's Greatest Gift (15 minutes). Ask a student to read aloud Ephesians 5:22–33. Again have the students discuss the questions on the student page. Discuss with the class the amazing model for relationships given in these passages.

Closing (5 minutes). Close with a group prayer. Ask students to pray specifically about relationships. Also thank God for His gift of sexuality and His strength to use it in a way that is pleasing to Him.

Extending the Lesson

- Have students brainstorm a list of television shows that depict couples and relationships. Discuss how these shows depict positive or negative values, based on what you've studied today.
- Invite a married couple to class to talk about their relationship. Focus on how they daily live out Paul's words in Ephesians 5.

A Precious Gift

1 For Adam and Eve

Read **Genesis 2:4–25.**

- What was God's purpose in uniting Adam and Eve?

- What kind of relationship did God desire between Adam and Eve?

- What role did God's gift of sexuality play in that relationship?

2 For Us

Read **John 8:1–11.**

- Of what sin was the woman accused?

- What was Jesus' attitude toward the woman?

- What message is Jesus sending to those who commit sins against the Sixth Commandment?

3 God's Greatest Gift

Read **Ephesians 5:22–33.**

- What model does Paul suggest to illustrate the love relationship of marriage?

- Both for those who marry and those who remain single, what great Gospel message is in these verses concerning Christ and the church?

- Give two or three helpful hints for newlyweds based on these verses.

3 The Blame Game

Genesis 3:1–24 (OLIC: September 17, 2000)

Purpose

Society often rationalizes sinful actions, blaming other people or things. In reality our sinful actions result from our sinful nature. The Good News is that Jesus has the cure for sin. He gives eternal life to all who believe in Him through the power of the Spirit.

Opening (5 minutes). Prior to the session gather several newspaper articles about examples of sin in society. As class begins, share these articles with the students and ask for their reactions. What other signs of sin do they see in the world? Have we become callous to sin, thinking of it as acceptable within our culture? Offer a brief prayer asking God's blessing on the session.

1. Three Scenarios (10 minutes). Distribute copies of the student page. Read and discuss each of the three scenarios. How did the people try to rationalize their sinful actions? What other excuses do people use to justify actions that go against God's will? What negative effect does rationalizing our sinful action have on our relationship with God?

2. Into the Word (15 minutes). Like contemporary people, Adam and Eve tried to play the blame game. But God would not allow that. He lovingly sought them out and, in spite of the consequences, gave them a reason to hope. Direct the students to Genesis 3:1–24. Ask a volunteer to read the verses aloud. Divide the class into small groups to discuss the questions found on the student page. Remind the students that while the serpent did tempt Eve, Adam and Eve decided to disobey God. In the same way, adults and teenagers need to assume responsibility for their bad decisions.

3. God's Loving Response (15 minutes). Remind participants that God showed He still cared about Adam and Eve by promising them a Savior and also providing for their physical needs. Ask how God shows He cares for people today. Direct the students to Romans 5:12–21 and ask a volunteer to read it aloud. Ask how, according to Romans 5, sin came into the world. How did God's grace enter into the world? As baptized children of God, why do these verses give us reason to celebrate?

Closing (10 minutes). Ask the students to follow along as you read Romans 6:1–7. Through Baptism, sin is put to death in our life and is replaced by new life in Christ. That renewal takes place on a daily basis as we come before God's throne of grace in confession and absolution. For the closing prayer, ask God to touch each member of the class on a daily basis, reminding them that they are His forgiven children.

Extending the Lesson

- Have students create bookmarks using verses from Romans 5. Cover them with clear adhesive paper. Have students use this in a book they see daily as a reminder of God's daily grace to us.

The Blame Game

1 Three Scenarios

Theo was an above-average student in chemistry, but he always seemed to do poorly on tests. He was frustrated because he knew some of his classmates often cheated to get better grades. When his friends approached him with a stolen copy of an upcoming test, Theo jumped at the chance to improve his grade. Theo didn't realize that the teacher had planted the test, hoping to catch dishonest students. When confronted, Theo explained, "Everyone cheats. I was just trying to get the grade I deserve."

Connie often spent Saturday afternoon at the mall with her friends. One Saturday her friend Shelly suggested that they shoplift some cosmetics from a department store. Her other friend, Wendy, quickly agreed. When Connie objected, the girls made fun of her. Connie eventually gave in because she was afraid of losing her friends. The girls got caught, and the store turned the girls over to their parents. When her mother confronted her, Connie said, "It was Shelly and Wendy's idea. They made me to do it."

Conrad's parents divorced when he was very young. With his mother working long hours, Conrad had a lot of free time. His mother was always tired when she was home and his dad, an alcoholic, didn't care. In middle school Conrad started hanging out with a "bad" crowd. In high school he and several of his friends were arrested for destructive vandalism. When questioned, Conrad was quick to point out that he would never amount to anything because he came from a lousy home.

2 Into the Word

Read **Genesis 3:1–24.**

- What motivated Eve and Adam to eat the forbidden fruit?

- What role did the serpent play?

- What were the consequences of Eve and Adam's decision?

- How does their decision affect us today?

God's Loving Response

Read **Romans 5:12–21.** What Good News does Paul remind us of, even though we are sinful?

4 I'm So Angry!

Genesis 4:1–16 (OLIC: September 24, 2000)

Purpose

In this lesson, students will explore the things that make them angry. They will be led to see how forgiveness offered through Christ's death and resurrection allows us to put aside anger.

Opening (10 minutes). Ask your students, "Whom have you been jealous of? Why were you jealous of that person? What made you want to be like that person or have what they had?"

1. Sibling Rivalry (15 minutes). Have students read Genesis 4:1–16 out loud. What is the theme of this text? Record their answers. (If envy, anger, or punishment are not offered as answers, suggest these as themes and encourage discussion about them.) Have students work through the questions on the student page. Ask volunteers to share their answers. As you discuss, point out that sin can begin small, but it grows and becomes deadly. Read James 1:14–15 and discuss the progressive steps of sin shown there.

2. Sin Solution (15 minutes). Thanks be to God that He sent His Son to rescue us from sin and its results. Have groups of students read the provided Scripture passages and discuss what each one says about sin and God's forgiveness.

- Psalm 1:1–3
- Proverbs 28:13–14
- Isaiah 43:25
- Luke 5:20–24
- 1 John 1:8–9

Allow volunteers to share their group's discoveries. Then invite volunteers to suggest ways we can respond in our lives of faith, especially in situations that threaten to make us angry.

Closing (5 minutes). Close with prayer, asking the Lord to forgive sins, both remembered and forgotten. Ask for strength to resist temptation and forgive those who anger us.

Extending the Lesson

- Not all anger is sinful. Anger can be driven by righteousness. Have students review the story of Jesus clearing the temple in John 2:13–17.

I'm So Angry!

Sibling Rivalry

Think about someone who makes you angry.
What is it about that person that makes you angry?

Read **Genesis 4:1–16.**

- Why was Cain angry with Abel?

- Why was God angry with Cain?

- In what ways are we like Cain?

- There were consequences for Cain's sin.
  What were they?
  What are the consequences for our sin?

Sin Solution

- **Psalm 1:1–3**

- **Proverbs 28:13–14**

- **Isaiah 43:25**

- **Luke 5:20–24**

- **1 John 1:8–9**

By Faith

Genesis 6:1–9:17 (OLIC: October 1, 2000)

Purpose

Christian young people are eager to know God's will for their lives. Today's lesson will focus on how we live by faith in the grace of God.

Opening (10 minutes). Ask students to share a time they have been asked to do something that didn't make sense. What was it? Who asked them to do it? If they were one of Noah's sons, would they have remained faithful to the project God placed before Dad, or would they have left because they thought he was crazy or because of the taunting of the people around them?

1. The Remarkable Ark (15 minutes). Most students will be familiar with the story of Noah and the flood. Introduce the story by reading Genesis 6:11–7:5. Have students work together to answer the questions from the student page. Discuss their answers.

(The ark was about one and two-thirds football fields long, one full-sized basketball court wide, and five and a half stories high. Noah took more of the clean animals because he needed to have animals for food and for an offering to God. The clean animals were those acceptable for eating under Jewish dietary laws. The unclean animals were needed to repopulate the earth. Noah lived in a desert region without many trees. There were no cranes or power tools for assembling the ark. Noah did everything as God had commanded.)

2. Get on Board (10 minutes). Have the students read 2 Peter 2:5. Allow the students to work together to answer the questions from the student page. (In the time leading up to the flood, Noah was busy preparing the ark, loading supplies and animals, and worshiping God. Life on the ark was probably kept busy with the activities of daily living, plus caring for their cargo. Given the lack of many windows and the rain, it was probably fairly dark inside the ark.)

3. Rainbow Remembrances (10 minutes). Have students read the verses from the student page and discuss their findings.

Review God's promise to Noah and his family in Genesis 8:21–22 and Genesis 9:8–17. What promises does God make to His people? (God promised to never again curse the ground and never to destroy the earth with a flood again. As a further sign of His promise and covenant with mankind, God used the rainbow as a reminder that He would never again destroy the earth with a flood.)

Closing (5 minutes). Close in prayer, thanking God for the Old Testament faithful and the example they set for us. Thank God for sending His Son to complete the work of salvation for us.

Extending the Lesson

• Have groups create a skit of a television news team interviewing the "crew" of the ark after they have made a sacrifice to the Lord. The skit could be presented to the class.

• Read together Hebrews 11:1–40. Create a "Faith's Hall of Fame." Teams of students could write citations (and create plaques) for each "hero of faith."

By Faith

1 The Remarkable Ark

Read **Genesis 6:11–7:5.**

• Given the dimensions of the ark, what could you compare it to?

• What details of the ark surprise you?

• Why do you think Noah was supposed to take only one pair of the unclean animals and seven pairs of the clean animals?

• What difficulties do you suppose Noah faced in building the ark?

• What words remind us of Noah's acceptance of God's direction?

2 Get on Board

Read **2 Peter 2:5.**

• What might Noah have been doing up until the time God closed the door to the ark?

• Based on what you've read, what was life on the ark like?

3 Rainbow Remembrances

Noah was rescued through God's grace from a world drowning in sin, floating through the flood in the ark. What does God promise His people about His future treatment of sinful people? (See **Genesis 8:21–22** and **9:8–17.**)

How did God fulfill that covenant promise? (See **1 Peter 3:18–21.**)

Read **Hebrews 11:7, 39–40.** What really saved Noah? What does God have in mind for you?

6 Get Moving

Purpose

God desires to guide us as we listen to Him. As we follow His leading, we receive His blessings as well.

Opening (10 minutes). Have a world or regional map displayed in the classroom when the students arrive. Ask the students to use push pins (or self-stick notes) and yarn or string to identify where they came from and places they have been. Discuss how they came to be at this place, how they traveled, and who guided them here. (If a map is not available, students can use the map on the student page.)

Follow up by asking, "Whom do you ask for directions to get somewhere you haven't been before? How do you know these directions are reliable?" Help students see that the best directions come from those who have experience or knowledge.

1. Address Unknown (15 minutes). We are not the only ones who have traveled without knowing where we were going. Read the story of Abram in Genesis 12:1–9. Have the students complete the questions on the student page. Discuss their answers. Why is it sometimes harder for us to obey God than it was for Abram? (Sin.) God led Abram to obey His commands, strengthened Abram through trials, and blessed him in many ways. How has God promised to bless us as we follow Him? Why? (Help the students understand that God's blessings are not offered as an inducement to get us to follow Him. God works faith in our hearts, empowers us by His Spirit to follow Him, and blesses and supports us along the way because He loves us.)

2. Lead the Way (10 minutes). God speaks to us today through His Word. Have students read the verses listed on the student page. What do each of these verses tell us about God's leading? Look at Jeremiah 3:14–15. Who are some of the "shepherds" God has put in your life? How can they help us?

Direct students to read James 3:17. Discuss each of the qualities mentioned in the verse as they relate to wisdom (pure, peace-loving, considerate, submissive, full of mercy and good fruit, impartial, and sincere). Have the students remember these traits as they consider the questions concerning selecting a college on the student page.

Closing (5 minutes). God wants us to follow Him. He knows the way and how we should get there. He has provided us His Word, His Holy Spirit, pastors, parents, and others to help in knowing His will. Pray: "Lord God, thank You for all the ways You help me follow You. Help me to not only listen to You but follow You like Abram did long ago. Amen."

Extending the Lesson

- Have students consider ways that they can invite teens who are new to the community to be part of the youth group.
- Prepare a "welcome" package for new people in the community or church.

18

GET MOVING

1 Address Unknown

Read **Genesis 12:1–9** and answer the following questions.

- How did Abram know it was the Lord talking to him?

- Why did it take a great deal of faith for Abram to follow God's leading? Where did that faith come from?

- What promises did God make to Abram?

2 Lead the Way

What does each of the verses tell us about God's leading?

- **Psalm 32:8**

- **Psalm 143:10**

- **Revelation 7:17**

- **Jeremiah 3:14**

Consider the traits listed in **James 3:17** as you consider these questions concerning choosing a college or university to attend.

- Is it a *pure* university?

- Are its faculty and campus *peaceable*?

- Are the faculty and people *considerate*?

- Are the courses and requirements *reasonable*?

- Can you be full of *mercy* and *good fruit* there?

- Could you be *impartial* and *sincere* when you attend there?

Just a Little Closer

Genesis 18:16–19:26 (OLIC: October 15, 2000)

Purpose

The student will learn how associations with people can and will affect their other relationships, especially their relationship with God. Yet God is unchanging in His care for them.

Opening (5 minutes). Have the room ready *before* the students appear. Arrange the chairs closer to you than usual. On one chair in the room, place something unpleasant (moldy food or dirty socks). Make sure the students can see it. As the students enter, note their reactions. Continue to make small talk as they settle in. Notice how some will sit next to the unpleasant item (don't allow it to be moved) while others may refuse to be anywhere near it. When class begins, take the unpleasant item away.

(As a less active, alternative opening, ask students to rank the following on an unpleasantness scale of one to ten, with ten being the most unpleasant:

____One-month-old gym-locker clothes
____School lunches
____That fast-food sandwich that's been in your car since last week
____Putting in someone else's retainer
____Noticing food in your date's teeth
____Forgetting your antiperspirant.)

Read Psalm 1:1–2 aloud. Discuss how students reacted to the unpleasant object(s). Discuss how they initially felt about the object and how their attitudes changed.

1. The First Step (10 minutes). Have a volunteer read Genesis 13:8–13. Point out that as Lot exercised the choices he had of where to live, his choices changed. Can the students see the progression? He lived with Abram until there were problems. When Abram asked him to pick an area of land in which to live, Lot chose the fertile lands inhabited by many other people, including residents of Sodom and Gomorrah. Later in Genesis we find Lot living *in* Sodom. He had gotten closer and closer, until he was living among some very sinful people. Have students complete the questions on the student page. Discuss their answers.

2. Too Close (10 minutes). Divide Genesis 18:16–19:26 into sections. Assign sections to students to read and summarize the story for the group. Remind students that Abram is now Abraham, having made a covenant with God. After summarizing the story, have students complete the questions on the student page. Discuss students' findings.

3. Up Close and Personal (10 minutes). Have students respond to the first question. Listen carefully for points to discuss further. Ask students to read the verses listed and summarize God's message to us. Be sure to emphasize the wonderful words of promise in Psalm 51.

Closing (5 minutes). Close with a group prayer. Ask students to include any special petitions. Conclude by thanking God for always renewing our spirit through His grace.

Extending the Lesson

- With students' help, develop a list of great Scripture verses of God's promise to be near us.

Just a Little Closer

1 The First Step

- According to **Genesis 13:8–13**, why was Lot attracted to the area around Sodom?

- Why do you think Lot chose to move into the city?

2 Too Close

- In **Genesis 18:16–33** it appears that Abraham is negotiating with God. Why do you think Abraham was so persistent?

- What message is there for us about boldness in prayer?

- Without being too graphic, give some examples from **Genesis 19:1–17** that show how bad things were in Sodom.

- How does God demonstrate His care for Lot?

3 Up Close and Personal

What modern equivalents of "Sodom" do we find ourselves in the middle of?

Read each of these verses and summarize God's message to us.

- **Psalm 1:1**

- **1 Corinthians 15:33**

- **Psalm 51:7–12**

8 Tested to the Limit!

Genesis 22:1–19 (OLIC: October 22, 2000)

Purpose
Young people find their values and beliefs tested daily. This session reveals that faith in Jesus Christ gives God's people the ability to endure those times of testing.

Opening (5 minutes). As students arrive, see who can hold their breath the longest. Time each person. Talk about how to improve on this skill. Ask if there is a limit to how long people can hold their breath.

1. How Far Would You Go? (10 minutes). Distribute copies of the student page. Every person has limits for behavior. Your students just won't do certain things! Explore some of those limits. Direct the students to the statements on the student page. Ask them to place an X in the column that best defines their limit for each issue. Give students time to respond. Discuss their choices.

Then ask, "Have your limits on these issues always stayed the same? Which have changed? Why? Which might change in the future? Why? Are you ever tempted to go past your limit in these or other areas? Explain."

2. To the Mountaintop! (10 minutes). Introduce the Bible study: "Abraham was a very important person in the history of our salvation. And yet God tested his faith. Today we explore Genesis 22 to learn more."

Read Genesis 22:1–19 and discuss the questions on the student page with the class. (Human sacrifice was not uncommon in early Old Testament times. Isaac had been promised by God and was special to God's plan for His people. The ram foreshadowed Jesus. Jesus died for us on the cross. In both cases, God acted in love and grace for His people!)

3. Test Preparation (10 minutes). Discuss preparations for times of testing. Point out that it is important to get ready for tests. The students may soon be tested with issues like those discussed earlier. How does one face times of testing?

Have the students read Hebrews 11:17–19 and answer the questions from the student page. Discuss their answers.

Have the students read James 1:12 and share their answers to the questions.

Closing (10 minutes). Ask students to complete the "To Think About" statement. After students are finished, close with a group prayer that allows each person to ask God to help with one issue.

Extending the Lesson
- Ask students to compare Jesus' suffering and death with Isaac's experience when the ram was substituted as a sacrifice. How are God's love and grace shown?
- Talk with students further about making God-pleasing decisions. Pray with them personally. Follow up one-on-one.

Tested to the Limit!

1 How Far Would You Go?

Place an X in the column that best defines your limit on the issue.	Likely to Do	Might Consider	No Way!
Yell at my parents			
Lie to protect a friend			
Cheat on a test			
Experiment with drugs or alcohol			
Engage in sex before marriage			
Skip school			
Go to an R-rated movie without telling my parents			
Shoot a person			
Keep $20 found near the grocery checkout			
Sell drugs			

2 To the Mountaintop!

Read **Genesis 22:1–19**.

• How did God test Abraham?

• Why do you think God asked this sacrifice of Abraham? Was it an unusual request?

• What is significant about the way that God resolved the situation?

• How did God provide for your sacrifice for sin?

3 Test Preparation

Read **Hebrews 11:17–19**. What was Abraham's source of strength?

• How can faith help you handle tests in life?

Read **James 1:12**. Who are the "blessed"?

• How are they "blessed"?

To Think About: The issues where my limits are being tested right now and where I need God's help are . . .

9 Telling His Story

Genesis 24:1–67 (OLIC: October 29, 2000)

Purpose

This lesson encourages young people in their faith and helps them tell their personal stories of God's loving actions in their lives.

Opening (5 minutes). As students arrive, begin generating a list of the "Top Five Things High School Students Like to Do." Post the completed list to be used later.

1. Telling Your Story (15 minutes). We all share many common experiences in life. But what makes them special is what happened to *you!* Let the students tell their stories. Have students work in pairs. Give directions and allow time for sharing.

1. Ask each student to choose one item from the "Top Five" list and share briefly about the best time they had doing that activity. Allow one minute for one student to share, then reverse roles and let the other person share for one minute.

2. Ask each student to choose one item from the "Telling Your Story" section of the student page. They should share briefly about the first time they ever did that activity. Give each student one minute to share.

3. Ask each student to share briefly about something God did in their life this past week. Again, allow one minute for each person.

Say, "Why can it be harder to talk about what God is doing than about what we like to do? Telling about school activities and life events can often be easier than telling about God's actions. Today we'll see that God's actions give us a story to tell."

2. With Eyes Wide Open (15 minutes). Read aloud the opening paragraph of this section on the student page. Then read each portion of Genesis 24 and discuss the questions as a class. Ask the students, "If you had been Abraham's servant, would you have had faith in God? Why?"

Invite students to look briefly at a New Testament story from Acts 4. Read together verses 1–3 and ask what message the disciples proclaimed. Why were they jailed?

Read verse 20 and discuss the disciples' explanation for their actions.

Read verse 33. Even after they had been arrested and jailed, what did the apostles persist in doing?

God acted in our lives through the suffering, death, and resurrection of Jesus Christ. By the power of the Holy Spirit, He continues to act today so we can tell His story.

3. Do You See Him? (15 minutes). Encourage students to share God's actions in their lives and to practice telling His story. Remind students that God uses His Word and Sacraments as means of grace—specific ways in which He intersects with our lives through His Spirit. Prayer is our means of communicating our needs to Him. Our family and others provide the community in which faith is taught. God's power and faithfulness are on display within nature. Encourage the students to choose one or more of the "story starters," make some notes about how God is active in their life, and share their story with a partner.

Closing (5 minutes). Close by reading Psalm 146 responsively by whole verse.

Extending the Lesson

- Have students write an essay on God's actions in their lives. Share the essays in future class sessions.
- Encourage students to "tell their story" this week to someone who is not a Christian. Ask them to report back next week.

Telling His Story

1 Telling Your Story

Let me tell you about the first time I ...

cooked a meal	scrubbed a toilet
acted in a drama	did the wash
changed a diaper	played in a concert
broke a bone	drove a car

3 Do You See Him?

Abraham's servant saw God act in a search for a bride. The apostles saw Him alive from the tomb. They all had a story they told over and over to all who were near. Tell some of the stories of God's action in your life. How does God act for you . . .

- in your Baptism and in Holy Communion?

- through Bible study?

- in response to prayer?

- through your family and others?

- within nature?

2 With Eyes Wide Open

As Abraham's life drew to a close, he directed his chief servant, probably a man named Eliezer, to find a bride for his son Isaac. This bride would not be from among local pagans, but from among Abraham's relatives in Mesopotamia. Abraham's faith in God was certain. Check out the story of his success.

- Read **Genesis 24:7–9**. Abraham had faith! Did his servant?

- Read **Genesis 24:10–14**. Whose help did the servant seek? What did he ask for?

- Read **Genesis 24:15–21**. Who was Rebekah? Was all of this pure luck? Why?

- Read **Genesis 24:22–27**. Why did the servant bow down and worship God on the spot?

- Abraham's servant recognized God's action in his life. He responded in worship and in what other way? (See **verses 33, 48,** and **50–51.**)

Scan the events of **Acts 4.** Look for similarities to **Genesis 24.**

10 The Right Light

Genesis 25:19–34; 27:1–29 (OLIC: November 5, 2000)

Purpose
Our sinful nature will always choose instant gratification without regard for long-term cost or consequences. As Jesus lives in us through Word and Sacrament, we are able to make choices that are guided by spiritual concerns.

Opening (5 minutes). Create a poster announcing a contest. The winner can choose to receive $1,000 instantly or $100 a month for a year. Ask which prize the students would choose. Why did they make that choice?

1. Thinking about Light (15 minutes).
Distribute copies of the student page. Give the students five minutes to list the positives and negatives of buying a $100 car.

Invite volunteers to share their responses and write them on the board or newsprint. Remind students of the hidden costs like insurance, maintenance, and gasoline. Help the students see that a cheap car will have good and bad consequences.

Have the students consider who might be affected by the decision to buy the car. How will this affect their uncle, parents, friends, and siblings? Help the students explore how their decisions have long-term effects on others.

2. Seeing the Light (20 minutes).
This section focuses on the choices Esau (Genesis 25:27–34) and Jacob (Genesis 27:1–29) made, and God's grace toward them despite bad choices. Have the students read Genesis 25:27–34 aloud. Read and discuss the questions on the student page. Then ask how God helps us even when we make bad decisions.

Have the students read Genesis 27:1–29 as a drama with parts for Isaac, Rebekah, Jacob, Esau, and a narrator. Discuss the questions on the student page. Also ask what effect this trick might have had on the relationships between Jacob and Isaac, and Esau and Rebekah. How did God bless these people in spite of their sin?

3. Bringing the Light (10 minutes).
We often make choices without thinking of the cost in the future. Ask the students, "When are you more likely to act on impulse rather than with lots of thought?" Discuss the Bible passages and questions on the student page. Assure the students that God is at work in their lives, empowering them to make wise decisions because He loves them.

Closing (5 minutes). Hand out index cards to each student. Have students write on the card a decision they are facing in the next month and a possible solution for the decision. Encourage them to write two positives and two negatives about this decision. Close with a prayer asking for God's wisdom and help with the decision.

Extending the Lesson
• Read 1 Kings 3:1–15 to see how young Solomon faced a time of tough choices. Make a list of what was most important to Solomon. List the blessings the Lord gave him for his long-term thinking.

26

The Right Light

1 Thinking about Light

Your uncle just bought a new car. You would like to buy your uncle's old car for $100. List below the long-term positive and negative consequences of buying this car.

Positives	Negatives

2 Seeing the Light

Read **Genesis 25:27–34**. What was Esau's immediate need? What did Jacob demand in trade?

What was the birthright? (See **Genesis 25:5**.) How might its value compare to that of stew?

Suppose you were Esau. What would you have done when Jacob had demanded such a high price for stew?

Read **Genesis 27:1–29**. What did Rebekah want for Jacob?
Do you think the success of the plan meant God really approved?

Read **Genesis 27:41–44**. What was the ultimate cost for Jacob's success? Do you think his success was worth it?

3 Bringing the Light

- Why do *we* make bad choices, decisions that result in harm to us or others?

- Read **Romans 7:21–25** and **1 Peter 2:9**. What hope is there when we feel trapped by our sinful nature in bad choices?

11 God Is My Protector

Genesis 28:10–33:20 (OLIC: November 12, 2000)

Purpose

In our mobile society, it is comforting to know that God protects us from danger. In this lesson we will explore God's provision and protection wherever we go.

Opening (5 minutes). Post a map of a distant place you have been or share pictures from that location. Ask the class what is the farthest they have ever traveled from home and if they had any problems or fears on the trip.

1. Thinking about It (15 minutes). Distribute copies of the student page. Tell the group to plan a camping trip. Give the students five minutes to list all needed supplies. Write student answers on the board. (Encourage them to remember sleeping, clothing, food, cooking equipment, tents, and even transportation needs.) What things could go wrong? Talk about the possible dangers on a long journey.

Ask, "How would you guard against those kinds of dangers?" (Some of the supplies they have listed might prevent certain dangers.) "How could God help? In what ways might we ask God to be part of our trip?"

2. Seeing the Light (20 minutes). Have the students read Genesis 28:10–22 aloud. Read the questions from the student page and have the students take turns responding. Help the students see the many promises and undeserved blessings God gives to Jacob. Where do you see amazement in Jacob's response? Where do you see Jacob express some doubt? Encourage the students to share a time when God exceeded their expectations.

Read Genesis 29:14–30 aloud. Work through the questions on the student page. Laban at first seems to be a model relative, but we later see another side of his personality. Encourage the students to explore the viewpoint of the two daughters who are treated as property. Explore what their relationship with their father might be after this incident.

3. Bringing the Light (10 minutes). Direct the students to the verses on the student page. Have students read and summarize the promises in each verse. Have the students describe ways that God is trustworthy and how He helps us when we need Him.

Closing (5 minutes). Reread the promise in Genesis 28:15. Have students discuss how they feel knowing that God protects them in danger. Close with a prayer thanking God for being trustworthy in every situation.

Extending the Lesson

• Have students list promises that God makes to His people throughout the Bible. Tell how each of these promises was fulfilled, keeping 2 Corinthians 1:18–20 in mind.

God Is My Protector

1 Thinking about It

List the supplies needed for a one-week camping trip.

List some things that could go wrong on the trip (car breaks down, food spoils, etc.).

Put an **X** by items that might help you if there is trouble.

2 Seeing the Light

Read **Genesis 28:10–22**. What are some potential dangers for the journey? What are some of the promises God makes to Jacob? What does God ask in return?

How does Jacob respond? When has God exceeded your expectations?

Read **Genesis 29:14–30**. How might Jacob have seen Laban before and after this story?

How do you think Rachel or Leah felt about their deceptive dad, Laban?

How and why is trust in God better than trusting other people?

3 Bringing the Light

- **Proverbs 3:5–6**
- **Isaiah 43:1–3a**
- **John 16:24**
- **1 John 1:9**

Read **2 Corinthians 1:18–20**. How are promises fulfilled in Jesus Christ? What does this mean for us? List some ways that God helps you each day. What else might you ask Him to do?

12 Betrayed and Befriended

Genesis 37:1–36; 39:1–41:57 (OLIC: November 19, 2000)

Purpose

Young people experience betrayal in their relationships. In this lesson students will learn that God befriends us and never will betray us. Through the Spirit, He empowers us to forgive those who betray us.

1. If … (5 minutes). Have students suggest a situation where someone might be betrayed. Invite students to role-play the event. Say, "Share a time when you were helped by a friend or a sibling. When you are in trouble, what person do you most often count on? Has this person ever betrayed you?" Distribute copies of the student page. Allow students time to complete the three sentences on the student page. Invite volunteers to share their answers.

2. I Can't Believe They Did This! (15 minutes). Assign individuals or groups to summarize the Bible cases of betrayal. Ask, "How might these experiences have changed Joseph? Do you think people generally grow closer to God because of their trials, or do they turn away from Him? Defend your answer."

3. God to the Rescue (10 minutes). Assign individuals or groups to read the Bible accounts and summarize how God befriended Joseph. Read Romans 8:28 aloud. Say, "God promises to bring good from our troubles, but He does not promise to take all our troubles away. Why not? How was this true for Joseph? How do you suppose Joseph might have been changed because of his troubles?"

4. I'm the Forgiven Betrayer (10 minutes). Have volunteers read the verses aloud. Discuss the questions on the student page. Help students to understand that our salvation does not depend on what we do, but on what Jesus did for us when He willingly gave up His life, taking the punishment for our sins.

5. My Turn to Forgive (10 minutes). Have volunteers read the verses aloud. Say, "Why is it so hard to forgive? Our sinful nature always desires to take revenge, so we cannot forgive without God's help. But as the Holy Spirit works faith in our hearts, He transforms us so we become more like Jesus and are able to forgive. When we forgive, it heals us as well as the person who is forgiven."

Closing (5 minutes). Invite students to pray silently for someone who has hurt them and to ask for God's help to forgive. Lead the class in this prayer:

"Dear Jesus, Forgive me for the times I have betrayed You, especially when I have not forgiven those who hurt me. Send Your Holy Spirit to transform me so I can be more like You. I pray in Your name, Jesus, knowing You love me unconditionally and answer every prayer. Amen."

Extending the Lesson

- Jesus knew ahead of time that He would be betrayed. How did He treat His betrayer (Matthew 26:20–25, 49–50)?
- Have students cite biblical examples of people befriending their enemies. (See Luke 10:33–35; 23:34, 40–43; Acts 7:59–60.)

Betrayed and Befriended

1
If …

- If my brother was jealous of me, he might …

- If I was falsely accused of something, my friends would …

- If I was betrayed by my family and friends, I would …

2
I Can't Believe They Did This!

How was Joseph betrayed

- by his brothers? (Genesis 37:12–36)

- by his master's wife? (Genesis 39:7–20)

- by his fellow prisoners? (Genesis 40:1–23)

3
God to the Rescue

How did God befriend Joseph in his troubles

- while he was a slave? (Genesis 39:2–6)

- while he was a prisoner? (Genesis 39:21–23)

- when he was called before Pharaoh? (Genesis 41:9–57)

4
I'm the Forgiven Betrayer

How have we betrayed God? How does He befriend us?
- Romans 6:23

- Ephesians 2:1–5

5
My Turn to Forgive

How can we befriend those who betray us?
- Ephesians 4:32
- 1 Thessalonians 5:15–18

13 Heart Check

Genesis 42:1–45:28; 50:15–21 (OLIC: November 26, 2000)

Purpose

Many young people carry a burden of guilt, while others feel no regret for their sins. In this lesson students learn how God helps us repent of our sin and then move beyond it as we trust Jesus to forgive us and help us live for Him.

1. It's Just a Test (10 minutes). Prepare samples of a popular brand and a generic brand of cola, peanut butter, or another product. Challenge students to identify the generic brand by looks alone. How can you test these products to find the differences? Allow students to sample the products and note the differences that can be found through a taste test. Discuss the questions on the student page.

2. Bruised by Sin (15 minutes). Read through the Bible references and answer the questions from the student page. Emphasize that Joseph may not have challenged his brothers out of revenge. He may have been testing them to see if they had repented of their sin or if they were the same hard-hearted brothers who ignored his cries and sold him into slavery years ago.

3. Healed by Forgiveness (15 minutes). Read and discuss the Bible references. Say, "What evidence do you see that Joseph still loves his brothers? How does forgiving someone who has not repented show love? Joseph knew God's forgiving love. Since he loved his brothers, he wanted them to know God's forgiveness too. If Joseph's brothers were not sorry and did not repent of their sin, they would not know God's forgiveness. Joseph lovingly did what he could to create a loving and forgiving relationship."

4. My Sin and God's Solution (10 minutes). After you read the verses about sin, allow time for students to reflect on the sin in their own hearts. Work through the remaining verses, emphasizing the words of God's forgiveness. Speak of the comfort God brings to each believer through faith in Jesus. Ask, "How does Satan use guilt to draw us away from God? Satan wins when we reject God's forgiveness and continue in our sin. God wants us to live joyfully, trusting Him to supply the grace to cover even our worst sins, as He helps us look forward to living in heaven with Him."

Closing (5 minutes). Ask students to skim Psalm 103 and identify phrases that assure them they are forgiven. If time is short, concentrate on verses 1–12. Close by reading the psalm, alternating by whole verse.

Extending the Lesson

- Discuss: Should a prisoner's lack of remorse for her crime be taken into account when she is being sentenced or considered for parole? When are feelings of guilt good? When are they harmful? For help see Psalm 32:3–5 and 1 John 1:8–10.
- Study together the Confession and Absolution portion of the liturgy. Ask, "Why is this part of the service so important? What feelings does it bring? Why?"

Heart Check

1 It's Just a Test

- What can you learn by taking a test? What can you learn by giving one?

- Why are tests so important at school? the hospital? factories?

2 Bruised by Sin

Joseph had been sold as a slave by his brothers. Most people would have thoughts of revenge or concerns for other members of the family. Why might each of these questions have gone through Joseph's mind? What do you think the answers might be?

- Are my brothers tormenting Benjamin now?

- Are they burdened with guilt?

- Have they forgotten what they did to me?

- How is my father?

- How will my life end up?

What test did Joseph give his brothers? **(Genesis 42:6–20)**

What was their response? **(Genesis 42:21–28)**

During the brothers' second visit to Egypt, Joseph wanted to observe their relationship with Benjamin. He tested them again.

- What were the tests? **(Genesis 4:34–44:17)**

- What did Joseph learn about his brothers? **(Genesis 44:18–34)**

3 Healed by Forgiveness

What did Joseph do when he saw his brothers' repentant hearts? **(Genesis 45:1–15)**

After their father died, the brothers were afraid Joseph would try to get revenge. They still had guilty hearts. How does Joseph reassure them? **(Genesis 50:15–21)**

Do you think Joseph would have forgiven his brothers if they were not sorry for what they had done? How does God create repentant hearts? How does that prepare us for the forgiveness He offers?

4 My Sin and God's Solution

What does God's Word teach us about our sin? **(James 4:17; 1 John 1:8)**

What does it teach us about forgiveness? **(1 John 1:9)**

Satan may tempt us to doubt God's forgiving love and wallow in our guilt. How do the following verses reassure us? **(Ephesians 2:4–5; 1 John 4:9–10)**

14 Preparing for God's Play

Esther (OLIC: December 3, 2000)

Purpose

Young people may think they are too young to serve God. This lesson helps them see that God has work for them to do *here* and *now*. God's will is done with or without them! He desires to involve them and share His blessings with them.

Opening (5 minutes). Pass around some news-magazines that focus on celebrities. Have students identify signs of good and bad in the celebrities' lives. Ask for other examples of people who were in the right place at the right time and became famous. What led to their fame? How is God involved when things look like luck or coincidence?

1. Preparing for the Task (10 minutes).

Ask students to respond to the choices on the student page. Then pose these questions:

- An athlete trains rigidly but sits on the bench. A fellow bench-sitter skips practices, then gripes that the coach is unfair. When an injured player needs replacing, which one of the bench-sitters do you think will be picked to play? Why?
- A musician practices several hours a day, dreaming of a solo opportunity. A fellow musician with much natural talent does not practice. Which do you think the music director will choose for the solo? Why?
- A medalist swimmer watches as someone struggles against the deadly current of the river. He has the ability to make the rescue, but he is not willing to do so. Would you risk your life to save someone you didn't know? Why?

Conclude by asking, "How might God lead a believer to act in each situation? What do Colossians 3:17 and Romans 12:3–8 say about our attitude and action in life situations?"

2. Looking into God's Word (20 minutes).

Class time will not allow for reading all 10 chapters of the Book of Esther. However, the instructor should be familiar with the entire story.

The story line should be easily understood by reading the following sections: 2:1–7, 17–23; 3:1–2, 5–6; and 4:1–17. Volunteers can read aloud or present a class drama with parts for a narrator, Haman, Mordecai, Esther, and King Xerxes.

Have students share their answers to the questions from the student page.

Focus on Esther 4:12–14. Discuss students' answers to the questions on the student page.

3. Carrying Out the Task (10 minutes).

Help students see their place in God's plan. Ask, "Is it coincidence that you are a Christian? Is it fate that you live where you live? Is it luck that your friends have you as a friend? How does God motivate Christians to meet others' needs? How does God equip believers for service to Him?"

Ask students to write down a friend's name on the student page. Remind them that this friend was put in their life by God's design. What does this friend need? Does this friend know Jesus as Savior? How can your students help? Fear may prevent us from serving others in God's name as led by the Holy Spirit. Have the class read 2 Timothy 1:7. Discuss how Jesus' grace overcomes fear. Discuss how 2 Timothy 2:20–21 describes us as God's instruments.

Closing (5 minutes). Invite students to pray for a friend. Have them ask for the Holy Spirit's guidance in discovering how God can use them to serve their friends and others.

Extending the Lesson

- Encourage students to write a list of strengths that God has blessed them with. Challenge them to be sensitive to their friends' needs and to consider how God desires to use them to share blessings with others.

Preparing for God's Play

1 Preparing for the Task

Circle those things that you feel lead to success.

luck	timing	good looks
location	coincidence	power
training	availability	position
God	fate	money
practice	recognition	friends

How does God define success? (See **Matthew 16:24–26**.)

What do **Colossians 3:17** and **Romans 12:3–8** say about our attitude and action in life situations?

3 Carrying Out the Task

God has given me a friend whose name is _____.

My friend knows/does not know Jesus as Savior.

My friend has this special need:

2 Timothy 1:7 reminds me:

I also remember God's purpose for my life (**2 Timothy 2:20–21**).

2 Looking into God's Word

Turn to the Old Testament Book of Esther. Read **2:1–7, 17–23; 3:1–2, 5–6; and 4:1–17.**

- What was Haman's evil plan?

- What was God's plan in this evil situation?

Look closely at **Esther 4:12–14**.

- How did Mordecai show faith that God would rescue the Jews?

- Was it coincidence that Esther was on the throne?

- What would God have done if Esther had remained silent?

- Whose power alone can overcome evil?

- In what ways was Esther's an earthly success story? In what ways might it be a spiritual success story?

15 *Preparing God's Way*

Malachi 3:1–4; Philippians 1:3–11; Luke 3:1–6 (OLIC: December 10, 2000)

Purpose

Teens may overlook the impact of their Christian witness upon their peers. This lesson reaffirms them as instruments of the Holy Spirit in preparing the way of Christ in the lives of others.

Opening (5 minutes). Discuss: In what way is the relationship of the advertising executive to producer, performer to songwriter, and ambassador to president similar to the relationship between the messenger and the source? Where else does this happen? What Bible stories describe how God brought people to faith? Ask the students to tell about when Christ first came into their lives. Who were the messengers of God's grace? What was the process? How do friends, parents, teachers, pastors, Holy Baptism, the Bible, church, and youth groups each influence their faith?

(This lesson builds on the premise that infant Baptism is a powerful way that Christ enters life through water and the Word. The Holy Spirit may often use events and other people as instruments that prepare someone's heart to receive the Gospel.)

1. Preparing the Way (10 minutes). Have students complete the matching activity on the student page. Prepare slips of paper that include a Bible reference about Gospel messengers on the inside fold and the student's name on the outside. These verses may include Matthew 28:18–20; John 3:5; John 3:14–15; John 3:16–18; Romans 8:16–17; Romans 8:37–39; Romans 10:8–15; Ephesians 2:8–10; Philippians 1:9–11; and 1 John 1:8–9. Have the students read aloud their Bible reference and briefly express what their passage says about the message or the messenger. Who is the messenger? What is the message? These verses contain God's message to them of His love and forgiveness. The means of grace—God's Word and Sacraments—proclaim God's message

with power. Any teacher or evangelist or servant merely serves as a messenger of God's love and forgiveness.

2. Looking into the Message (20 minutes). Advent is a time of preparation and expectation. Malachi 3:1–4 talks of a God-sent messenger who would prepare the way for the Messiah. Luke 3:1–6 shows the fulfillment of this prophesy through John the Baptizer. He was sent from God as a divine messenger to prepare people for Jesus, calling them to repentance for the forgiveness of sins (Luke 3:3). Help students learn more about the messenger and his message. Read Malachi 3:1–4 and Luke 3:1–6 to complete the questions from the student page.

3. Sharing the Message (10 minutes). Help the students see how they have been graciously called by the Gospel of Jesus Christ and claimed by the waters of Baptism. In Holy Baptism they have been marked as disciples of Christ to be His witnesses, His messengers. The work of God's messengers has not changed: it is to share God's message of salvation with others, preparing the way for Jesus to touch their lives. Let the students finish their section on "Sharing the Message."

Closing (5 minutes). Remind the students that God's messengers bring *God's* message, not their own. If a person rejects the messenger, then they are really rejecting God. Invite the students to pray that the Holy Spirit would use them as His messengers to share God's message about sin and grace with others.

Extending the Lesson

- Encourage the students to make a prayer list including their friends, classmates, workmates, or family members who need the life-changing power of Jesus' grace. Encourage them to identify specific ways that the Holy Spirit would use them as His messengers.

Preparing God's Way

1 Preparing the Way

Match each occupation with the most accurate description:

1. A teacher   a. shares a personal interview about a situation.

2. A weatherman   b. proclaims God's Word.

3. A messenger   c. publicly shares the news channeled to him.

4. A reporter   d. warns of an approaching storm front.

5. A preacher   e. instructs others with information on a subject.

6. An anchorman   f. delivers special news from one person to another.

2 Looking into the Message

In **Malachi 3:1** …

- Who is the Sender?

- Whose message was to be proclaimed?

- What was to be the work of the messenger?

In **Luke 3:1–6** …

- Who was God's promised messenger?

- In what location did he share the message?

- What was this message?

- What was the purpose for this messenger and this message?

- Has the purpose changed any today? Why or why not?

- What is the heart of the Gospel message? When is it most difficult to share? What might make it easier to be a messenger?

3 Sharing the Message

- Someone I know who needs Jesus is _____.

- Some excuses that person has for not wanting to be part of God's family or the church are …

- I can be God's messenger to this person by …

- As a messenger of God, when I read **Philippians 1:9–11**, I …

16 Real Christmas Gifts

Zephaniah 3:14–18; Philippians 4:4–9 (OLIC: December 17, 2000)

Purpose

The world's pleasures are shallow and short-lived. Everlasting joy is provided by God's grace, especially in His gift at Christmas of Jesus Christ.

1. Checking Out the Merchandise (10 minutes). Provide Christmas advertising circulars or rely on class members to know what's "hot" this year. Have students complete the wish list on the student page and share their choices with a partner. Discuss the other questions in this section. Invite students' comments and insights about "lasting gifts."

2. Sampling God's Gifts (20 minutes). Read Zephaniah 3:14–20. After picking out the obvious gifts of God listed here, discuss which are temporary and which are permanent, which are earthly and which are spiritual. Note that God's gifts last and, though they are spiritual gifts, they affect our everyday lives. Finally, show how these gifts are available only because of Christ's work of redemption and are received only by faith.

Read Philippians 4:4–9. Have students note the phrase *the Lord is near.* What does Paul have in mind? Apply their answers to the Christmas frenzy. How much of what we do actually indicates the nearness of God?

Allow students to complete this section and discuss their findings.

3. God's Gifts at Your House (10 minutes). Have each student describe a Christmas family tradition, suggesting how such traditions can serve to remind us of a blessing we have through Jesus Christ.

Closing (10 minutes). Have the students each write on a scrap of paper a specific spiritual gift (taken from Zephaniah or Philippians) that they would like to receive. No names attached. Redistribute requests and have each student pray for that gift.

Extending the Lesson

- Take Paul's list in Philippians 4:8 and plan a weeklong scavenger hunt; objects or reports are to be brought in next week. Challenge students to try to find something true, noble, right or correct, pure, lovely, admirable.
- Use the same list of gifts and discover how the world has taken God's gifts and turned them into opportunities to serve self.
- Which of our national traditions probably don't help to promote a spiritual emphasis? How could you change them?

Real Christmas Gifts

1 Checking Out the Merchandise

What's on your Christmas wish list this year?

List two or three items.

1.

2.

3.

Think back. What did you wish for last year? What was your favorite gift? Where is it now?

In the long run, what are the only gifts that really last?

2 Sampling God's Gifts

Read **Zephaniah 3:14–20**. List the items found on God's gift list.

- **Verse 15—**

- **Verse 16—**

- **Verse 17—**

- **Verse 18—**

- **Verse 19—**

- **Verse 20—**

Read **Philippians 4:4–9**. What do you think Paul means by the phrase *the Lord is near*?

How is the Lord near you, as expressed in verses **4, 6, 7, 8**?

What effect do these verses have on your preparations for Christmas?

3 God's Gifts at Your House

Which of your family Christmas traditions demonstrate God's real gifts of forgiveness and eternal life?

17 God, Understated

Luke 1:39–56; 2:1–20 (OLIC: December 24, 2000)

Purpose

God often chooses to do His work using normal people in quiet, unnoticed ways. Today's lesson looks at how God used such ordinary people to bring the Savior down to earth.

1. Getting Started (10 minutes). Have the students discuss the student page scenario—a Hollywood rewrite of God's original story of the birth of Jesus. Discuss the world's preoccupation with entertainment value, particularly that which appeals to our sinful human nature.

2. God at Work (20 minutes). Have volunteers read Luke 1:39–45. Mary's visit to her cousin Elizabeth and the reaction of Elizabeth's unborn child are all within the normal activities of people. But at the same time, God used these normal events to further the plan of salvation.

Read Luke 1:46–55. This song of Mary (called the Magnificat) was one of the early songs of the Christian church. Have the students pick out phrases that would be meaningful to a persecuted, struggling church. Point out that we experience similar situations and also need to hear God's message.

Read Luke 2:1–20. Many of your students could probably recite from memory this most famous of stories. Have them (with your help) point out how normal most of these events were (young couple expecting, crowded city, poor accommodations, birth, strange visitors). The one spectacular event was the message of the angels to the shepherds.

Have students share their observations. Focus the discussion on why God chose to bring His Son into the world in this way, rather than in ways Hollywood might invent. God came to humankind in a nonthreatening manner, in the form of a helpless infant.

The message of the angels was that through Christ, the warfare between God and humans was over. God had unilaterally, unconditionally, and at great cost ended it.

3. God at Work in You (15 minutes). Challenge the students to imagine that they are any of the people in the Christmas story (including Jesus). Have them tell what effect the coming of Christ in the flesh would have on them.

Encourage the students to consider sharing their own faith story. Help them see the events (Baptism, Bible study, Holy Communion, and others) and people (parents, sponsors, teachers, and friends) through which God has worked the miracle of Christ's coming in them.

Closing (5 minutes). Have the students write a one-line statement of praise similar to that of the angels' song, "Glory to God in the highest, and on earth peace to men on whom His favor rests" (Luke 2:14).

Extending the Lesson

- Have the students work together to write a modern magnificat to tell about what God has done in their lives.

40

God, Understated

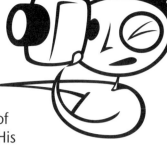

1 Getting Started

Suppose Matthew or Luke were to submit his account of the birth of Jesus to Hollywood for a made-for-television movie. What might the producers want to rewrite? Why?

2 God at Work

Read **Luke 1:39–45.** How did God use normal activities of normal people to accomplish His work?

Read **Luke 1:46–55.** Pick out examples of God's acts that the members of the early Christian church would eagerly remember.

Read **Luke 2:1–20.** In this well-known story, which events might have the only "Hollywoodlike" appeal? Why do you think God chose the shepherds to witness the message of the angels? Why do you think God chose to bring His Son into the world in this way?

3 God at Work in You

How did God work His plan of salvation in you?
What events resulted in your faith?
What people have shared His story with you?

18 Family Matters

Luke 2:41–52; Hebrews 2:10–18 (OLIC: December 31, 2000)

Purpose

Teens today are being bombarded with views of family that are far different from God's. In this session they will compare two families (their earthly family and their heavenly family) as they look at the life of Jesus.

Opening (10 minutes). Today there are many TV sitcoms portraying different types of families. Have the students discuss several of them. How do they portray relationships between parents? difficulties of one-parent families? teens living in a household with no parental guidance? children being raised by someone other than a parent?

1. Your Earthly Family (7 minutes). Distribute copies of the student page. Have students consider what they would like to see in their earthly families by completing the first section. Discuss their answers.

2. Your Heavenly Family (8 minutes). Now have students complete the set of questions for their heavenly family. They will have to adjust their thinking, since they are not the head of this family, but are instead one of the children.

Discuss their answers. Tell the students that they will see both types of families in the life of the 12-year-old Jesus.

3. Family Foundations (15 minutes). Read Luke 2:41–52 aloud. A growing number of children today have two fathers. Jesus' situation was different. His earthly father, Joseph (called "a parent" and "your father" in Luke 2), was not His birth parent. God Himself, through the Holy Spirit, conceived Him and was His true heavenly Father. Ask

the students to share their answers to the questions on the student page. (Mary and Joseph searched for Jesus until they found Him. Jesus' trip to Jerusalem fulfilled the obligation of the law, but it also became an opportunity for Him to begin to teach the truth of the Scriptures to the teachers in the temple.)

4. Bringing It Home (10 minutes). Read Hebrews 2:10–18 together. Allow students time to answer the questions on the student page. Encourage volunteers to share their answers. Spend time reviewing the words of verses 14–18. Help students see Christ's role in their salvation. (We are of the same family as Jesus, according to verse 11. Because Christ shared in our humanity, we share in His death and resurrection. It is because of His perfect keeping of the law that we are declared righteous.)

Closing (5 minutes). Lead the class in prayer, thanking God for families. Be sure to include a prayer of thanksgiving for the saving work of Jesus.

Extending the Lesson
- Refer to Matthew 12:46–50 and John 19:25–27 to see how Jesus responded to each of His families.

Family Matters

1 Your Earthly Family

How old do you want to be when you get married?

Will you want children?

How old do you want to be when you have your first child?

How many children would you like?

Put these qualities in the order that you would like to see them in your children (1—most important; 8—least important).

___ Respectful of authority

___ Having a good attitude

___ Smart

___ Healthy

___ Good-looking

___ God-loving

___ Obedient

___ Athletic

2 Your Heavenly Family

How did you become a member of God's heavenly family?

What is your role in the heavenly family?

What qualities do children of God have?

3 Family Foundations

Read **Luke 2:41–52**. List the things mentioned that showed Jesus had a loving and caring family here on earth.

What actions and words of Jesus tell us about His earthly and heavenly families?

What responsibilities to His heavenly Father and His earthly parents did Jesus carry out on this trip to Jerusalem?

4 Bringing It Home

Read **Hebrews 2:10–18**. What are we told about our relationship with Jesus? (**verse 11**)

Look closely at **verses 14–18**. What words tell us how much God cares for us? What has Christ done for us? Give examples of Jesus' human and divine natures from these verses.

19 Why Am I Here?

Luke 3:15–17, 21–22; Matthew 11:1–19; 14:1–12 (OLIC: January 7, 2001)

Purpose

God declared a specific mission for the life of John the Baptizer even before his birth. God has a specific purpose for our lives too, and He offers us His assurance and encouragement as we live for Him.

Opening (10 minutes). Before class, hide a treat, such as a bag of candy. Create a set of simple instructions to find the treasure. Then create a second set of instructions, leaving out key words so that the instructions will be impossible to decipher. Ask volunteers to accept the mission of finding what you have hidden, and provide the incomplete instructions. When they are stumped, ask them to read the instructions aloud. Point out that the volunteers lack enough information to complete their mission. Then give the volunteers the whole set of instructions and ask them to share the treat with the class.

1. Your Personal Mission Statement (10 minutes). Distribute copies of the student page. Talk about the popularity of mission statements. They can be found everywhere, from churches to fast-food restaurants. Challenge students to write a brief personal mission statement. Encourage them to share what they have written.

2. John's Mission Statement (15 minutes). Read aloud John the Baptizer's mission statement from Luke 1:17. These words were spoken to his father, Zechariah, by an angel. Direct students to complete this section of the student page, perhaps working in pairs or small groups. Then discuss the questions, bringing out these points:

In Luke 3:15–17, John denies being the Christ and boldly speaks of the one to come. When John baptizes Jesus (v. 21–22), God Himself identifies Jesus as His Son.

In Matthew 11:1–19, we find that John was imprisoned at this time for rebuking King Herod, who had divorced his wife to marry his brother's wife, Herodias (see Luke 3:19). Jesus reassures John not just with words, but with reminders of what He has done. Jesus also defends John to the people, calling him "the Elijah who was to come" (v. 14), and He rebukes the crowd for not accepting John's message or His own. In the last sentence of verse 19, Jesus tells the people that both John's message and His message will be proven true by action.

In Matthew 14:1–12, John is beheaded at Herod's party. This happened because John spoke the truth. Despite his untimely death, John had fulfilled his mission of pointing out the Christ.

3. God's Mission for Me (10 minutes). Have volunteers read the verses on the student page aloud and discuss what clues they give us about God's mission for our lives. Say, "God has told us that He has plans for our lives. Even though we may struggle to figure out the specifics of these plans, we all know that our main mission is the same as John's—to point others to Christ."

Closing (5 minutes). Close in prayer, asking God to guide your students as they seek His will in their lives. Also pray for strength in our common mission of pointing to Christ.

Extending the Lesson

- Work together to write a mission statement for your Bible class or youth group. Post it where your group meets.

Why Am I Here?

1 Your Personal Mission Statement

Why are you here? What goals do you have for your life? Use the space below to write a brief personal mission statement.

2 John's Mission Statement

Read **Luke 3:15–17, 21–22**. How did John make his mission clear to the people who wondered who he was?

John's mission was to point out the Messiah. How did this happen in Jesus' baptism?

John finds himself in prison and begins to have doubts about his mission. Read **Matthew 11:1–19**. What is John's question? How does Jesus reassure John? How does Jesus defend John's mission to the people?

John's mission comes to an abrupt end at a party one night. Read **Matthew 14:1–12**. What brought John to this fate? Had he fulfilled his purpose?

3 God's Mission for Me

What do the following verses say about God's mission for your life? How are these words encouraging?

- **Psalm 139:16**

- **Psalm 32:8**

- **Proverbs 16:3, 9**

- **Jeremiah 29:11**

20 Jesus: The Life of the Party?

John 2:1–11 (OLIC: January 14, 2001)

Purpose
Often our image of Jesus is of someone on a serious mission. This session reminds us that Jesus also took time to enjoy the common celebrations of life. In the same way, Jesus can bring joy beyond imagination into our daily lives.

Opening (5 minutes). Gather different pictures of Jesus from around your church or home. Ask students to identify the difference in how Jesus is depicted in each picture. Invite students to share how they most often picture Jesus and where that image came from.

1. Picture This (10 minutes).
Distribute copies of the student page. Give students a moment to read the options and select one or more of them. Discuss the reasons for their choices. Challenge them to think of biblical situations similar to those listed.

Say, "We usually don't think of Jesus dancing the night away at a wedding. We usually picture Him being on a serious mission. Today's lesson will remind us that our Savior also took time to celebrate and bring joy to our lives."

2. Jesus Celebrates (15 minutes).
Ask a volunteer to read aloud John 2:1–11. Use the questions on the student page to review the story. Explain that a wedding feast in Jesus' day was a big occasion, lasting up to a week. Running out of wine at the feast would have been a major humiliation. Jesus' miracle spared this family a good deal of embarrassment. Discuss why Jesus chose this as His first miracle and what it says about Him. How does this miracle show Jesus' care for the ordinary things in our lives?

Say, "Jesus' first miracle may not have been spectacular. But through it, Jesus reminds us that He is part of our daily lives. If He cares for the everyday things, how much more does He care for the important things?"

3. My Cup Overflows! (15 minutes).
Ask the students to note the water jars Jesus used for this miracle. These jars were used for the ceremonial purification of hands, which was an obligation of the Jews. Point out that Jesus turned something that was law into grace! Jesus took a reminder of the law and turned it into an example of His overflowing love for us.

Have students identify other accounts of God's overflowing goodness. Possible answers might include manna in the wilderness (Exodus 16), the feeding of the 5,000 (John 6:5–13), or the miraculous catch of fish (John 21:1–14).

Read the verses listed on the student page and discuss how they show the abundance of God's grace for us.

Closing (5 minutes). Provide a small reminder of Jesus' presence, such as a cross sticker, for students to place somewhere they see daily. Encourage this as a reminder of Jesus in their everyday lives. Invite the class to speak the words of Ephesians 3:20–21 together as a closing benediction.

Extending the Lesson
- Share a specific time in your life when you feel that God provided more than you asked. Encourage students to do the same. Challenge students to ask their family members to share such a time.
- Have students create an invitation for Jesus to attend an upcoming event to remind us that He is always present.

Jesus—The Life of the Party?

1 Picture This

If Jesus were on earth today, where do you picture Him being?
- ☐ Preaching at a large service
- ☐ Playing with children on the playground
- ☐ Leading a Bible class at our church
- ☐ Helping serve a meal at a homeless shelter
- ☐ Taking time alone to pray in a peaceful spot like a park or garden
- ☐ Having dinner at your home
- ☐ Dancing the night away at your cousin's wedding
- ☐ Healing patients at a local hospital
- ☐ Stopping a funeral to comfort the family and raise the dead loved one

2 Jesus Celebrates

Read **John 2:1–11**. Where was Jesus in this story?

- What problem came up?

- How did Jesus respond? What was the result?

This was Jesus' first miracle. Why do you think Jesus didn't choose something more dramatic, such as a healing, to make His "debut"? What does this miracle tell us about Jesus?

3 My Cup Overflows!

Look back at the story. What does the text tell us about the water jars Jesus used in this miracle?

The six water jars mentioned in the story probably held 20–30 gallons each. That would mean that Jesus provided 120–180 gallons of wine for the wedding feast! This was certainly more than enough to meet the need. Can you think of other stories in which God provided "more than enough"?

Read about God's overflowing goodness in the following verses:
- **Psalm 23**

- **Romans 15:13**

- **Ephesians 3:17–21**

Now to Him who is able to do immeasurably more than all we ask or imagine, according to His power that is at work within us, to Him be glory in the church and in Christ Jesus throughout all generations, for ever and ever! Amen. (Ephesians 3:20–21)

21 Resting in Jesus

Luke 10:38–42; Matthew 11:28 (OLIC: January 21, 2001)

Purpose

Some teens are driven to do many things for God. Jesus has done all that the Law requires of us and invites us to rest in Him, rather than strive by our own efforts to please Him.

Opening (5 minutes). Ask the students, "How much sleep do you get at night?" Wait for responses. Ask, "Do you ever take a nap to get extra sleep? If you do, how long do you sleep?"

1. The Need for Rest (15 minutes). Distribute copies of the student page. Allow time for the students to answer the questions about the need for rest. Invite volunteers to share their answers. Also invite them to share an example when their performance dropped or relationships were hurt by their being tired.

Then ask whether most people work too much or rest too much. Ask students to explain their choice. Then ask, "What does faith in Jesus have to do with rest?"

2. Rest in the Word (20 minutes). Ask students to follow along as you read aloud Luke 10:38–42. Read the quotes dramatically, as they might have been uttered. Allow the students to work in pairs to answer the questions from the student page. Have each pair share their answers with the group.

Read Matthew 11:28–30 aloud. Share how the Law is a heavy burden that makes us weary. You might want to share the cliché "There is no rest for the wicked." Trying to follow the Law for our salvation will not provide rest; we will always fail. What does Jesus promise to give to those who come to Him?

3. Rest in Jesus (5 minutes). Discuss when and how normal Christian activities, such as prayer, worship, witnessing, Bible study, and service, can become burdens that distract us from Jesus.

Ask the students to share their preferred definition of *rest* from the choices on the student page. Ask the students to tell what it means to rest in Jesus.

Closing (5 minutes). Pray aloud the following, pausing for students to silently pray: "Dear Father, forgive us when we, like Martha, get distracted and focus on our works for You. We list those areas now where we try to impress You. (pause) Spirit, remind us that Jesus has done all that's necessary for our salvation and nothing we can do will make us more pleasing in the Father's eyes. (pause) Jesus, we thank and praise You for obeying the Father, dying for us, and promising eternal rest with You someday. May we always rest in You and in what You have done for us. In Your precious name. Amen."

Extending the Lesson

- Psalm 62:1 reads, "My soul finds rest in God alone." Ask the students where people try to find rest apart from God.
- Ask the students to discuss how they and their families spend Sundays. Is it really restful? What could make it more restful?

48

Resting in Jesus

1 The Need for Rest

Why do you think God created a day for rest?

• What happens when you are tired and need rest?

• How do you feel?

• How well do you perform activities?

• How well do you relate to others, such as family and friends?

2 Rest in the Word

Read **Luke 10:38–42**. Describe how Martha must have felt.

When and where have you felt that way?

Verse 40 says Martha was "distracted." *Distracted* means "drawn away." Where should Martha have given her attention? What things led Martha to be "worried and upset"?

3 Rest in Jesus

Rest is

1. refreshing ease;
2. relief or freedom from anxiety;
3. to have tranquility or peace.

• Which definition of *rest* do you prefer? Why?

• What does it mean to "rest in Jesus"?

He's All That!

Luke 4:14–32 (OLIC: January 28, 2001)

Purpose

Teens are trying to figure out what kind of career, spouse, car, and lifestyle they need to make life complete. The purpose of this study is to help them see that a personal relationship with Jesus Christ guarantees everything they really need.

1. What If? (15 minutes). Distribute copies of the student page. Ask students to describe in the box their idea of a perfect life. When they are finished have them share their concepts, listing them on the board.

Then ask, "Which of the things listed might you lose if you were disabled and couldn't work anymore?" Direct students to cross off those things in their descriptions that other students mention, as you cross them off the master list. "How about the death of a spouse or children?" Ask them to cross off those items that include family. "What if war or a huge natural disaster destroyed your town?" Tell students to cross off all of the material items on their lists. Challenge your students with this question: "If a perfect life depends on these things, what happens when they are lost? Would joy and contentment be impossible?" Allow students to share their thoughts. Say, "Today we want to consider what really makes life complete."

2. Life with Jesus (25 minutes). Direct a student to read Luke 4:14–32. Ask students to complete the table on their sheets by giving examples of people in need today. Then ask them to list specific examples of how Jesus helps such people in the world today. (For example, "those in prison" might be anyone enslaved by an addiction or sin. Jesus helps by providing forgiveness and freedom from sin as well as resources to overcome addiction.) After completing the table, invite students to share their ideas. Ask what role God has prepared for the church and Christians to play in helping people today.

3. In My Life (10 minutes). Invite students to complete the phrase in the space on the student page. Have students share their answers. Conclude by having students pray for the person on their left that Jesus would help that person with their need.

4. The Bottom Line (5 minutes). Conclude the lesson by reminding students that a complete life is not found in material things or situations that can change. A complete life is found in the forgiveness of our sins and the new life given to us through the death and resurrection of Jesus Christ. At the bottom of the student page is a scrambled sentence. Challenge students to unscramble it to see a modern "proverb" based on John 14:6 (for example, *Jesus is life. All the rest is detail*).

Extending the Lesson

- Invite students to make a bumper sticker with the "proverb" on it and place it on a school notebook or inside their locker.
- Ask students to think of ways their friends need to hear the Good News, be set free, have their sight restored, or be released from oppression. Challenge them to pray for these friends and look for ways to serve them in Jesus' name.

He's All That!

1 What If?

In the box below, describe what you think a perfect life would include.

3 In My Life

Where I need Jesus in my life right now is …

2 Life with Jesus

Read **Luke 4:14–32**. Next to each phrase below, list people today whom you would think Jesus is referring to.

	When the Messiah Came	Contemporary Counterparts	How Does It Happen Today
Good news for the poor			
Freedom for prisoners			
Recovery of sight for the blind			
Release for the oppressed			

4 The Bottom Line

ussje si fiel. lal het ster si deilat.

23 Miracles: Magic or Message?

Luke 5:1–11 (OLIC: February 4, 2001)

Purpose

Jesus' miracles capture our attention and impress us with His divine power. This session encourages us to see God's redeeming purpose and message in these mighty acts.

Opening (10 minutes). Ask students if they believe miracles still happen. Discuss what a miracle is (a supernatural act or event that contradicts the laws of nature, an extraordinary event manifesting divine intervention in human affairs). Encourage students to share any examples of modern day miracles that they know or have heard of.

1. The Super and Natural Jesus (10 minutes). Distribute copies of the student page and ask a volunteer to read the opening paragraph. Record the miracles that students can recall. Ask, "Why do you remember these miracles?" Student answers will vary. We are impressed by supernatural events or demonstrations of power that are beyond our natural capacity. Why did Jesus do all these miracles? Allow students to share their answers and record key phrases.

2. The Message of Miracles (20 minutes). Ask a volunteer to read John 10:25, 37–38. Have students compare their reasons for Jesus' miracles to the purpose given by the apostle John. Jesus did miracles to demonstrate that He was using the power of God to do the will of God. We can see that message in any miracle Jesus does. Let's see what other messages Jesus gives us in the miracle we study today. Choose three volunteers to read Luke 5:1–11— one to read narrator parts, one to read the words of Simon Peter, and one to read the words of Jesus. Lead the class in answering the questions on the student page. Simon Peter called Jesus "Master" (verse 5) and obeyed because he respected Jesus' teaching and accepted His authority. But having seen Jesus' supernatural power at work in the spectacular catch of fish, Peter calls Him "Lord" (verse 8)! Part of the message of Jesus' miracle was "Don't rely on your own experience and wisdom. Rather listen to and obey Me so that I can make you fishers of men."

3. Because You Say So! (10 minutes). Have a volunteer read the statement from the student page. Assign the students a Scripture text to examine. Have them share what challenging direction Jesus gives us.

Closing (5 minutes). Invite each student to participate in the closing prayer, thanking God for the gift of His Son, our Savior, and seeking the Spirit's power to obey His will. Encourage the prayer leaders to pray for humility and courage for us to obey Jesus.

Extending the Lesson

- Challenge class members to look through the Gospels for miracles that were not on their list at the beginning of the lesson.
- Ask each class member to choose one of the miracles from the list made at the beginning of the lesson and study it more closely.

Miracles: Magic or Message?

1
The Super and Natural Jesus

Jesus was a natural man, just like you and me. But what made Him super was the fact that He was also truly God. He used the power of God that was His to do the will of the Father. In His three years of ministry, Jesus did at least 35 miracles, relying completely on His godly power. How many do you remember?

2
The Message of Miracles

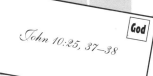
John 10:25, 37–38 — God

Jesus sent us a message in every miracle He performed. Go to the "address" on the envelope above to see what the apostle John tells us about Jesus' miracles.

Now read the account of one of Jesus' astonishing miracles in **Luke 5:1–11**.

There was no "common sense" reason for Simon Peter, an experienced and professional fisherman, to take Jesus' advice on how to fish! Why did he do it? And what did Peter learn from his act of obedience?

Was Jesus simply rewarding Peter for the use of his boat with that spectacular catch of fish? What was Jesus' message in this miracle?

3
Because You Say So!

Jesus told Peter to let down his net in water that he'd already fished in all night! Jesus calls us to be like Peter and ignore "common sense" and use instead our uncommon gift of faith.

Matthew 5:23–24

Matthew 5:38–42

Matthew 6:31–33

Matthew 11:28–30

John 15:9–12

24 Lord, If You Had Been There ...

John 11:1–46 (OLIC: February 11, 2001)

Purpose

Most believers can point to a time or experience when it seemed as if God just wasn't there. God promises that He will not leave or forsake His people. His Son, Jesus, was present for Mary and Martha, was present on the cross for us, and is present in our lives through the power of the Spirit.

Opening (10 minutes). Millions of people rely on 911 as the number to dial for emergencies. Ask the class to imagine that for one day the 911 system is out of service. What might happen during that day? In a crisis, people rely on more powerful or able people to rescue them.

1. Out to Lunch (10 minutes). Is God always there? Distribute copies of the student page and direct the students to fill in their answers for this section. Let volunteers share their examples.

2. Taking God Seriously (20 minutes). We are not the first people to feel as if God has overlooked them. Jesus' closest friends knew He was the Son of God, but they still felt He wasn't there for them. Ask volunteers to read aloud John 11:1–45. Consider reading it like a play.

Discuss the questions on the student page. Remind the students that Jesus was not ignoring His friends' plight. Jesus planned to do much more than heal a sick friend—He planned to demonstrate God's power and point people to God's kingdom.

3. Here Today—Here Tomorrow! (10 minutes). There's an old saying: "Here today, gone tomorrow." Jesus is not a fair-weather friend. What is really happening when we, like Martha and Mary, think God is ignoring our crisis? Let students answer. Direct the students to read Acts 18:9–10 and answer the questions on the student page. Let volunteers share their insights.

Closing (5 minutes). Direct the class to read aloud Acts 17:26–27 from the student page. These words remind us of God's care for His people throughout time. Lead the class in a prayer of thanksgiving for the special people named by class members as special agents of God.

Extending the Lesson

- Suggest that students study Jesus' prayer in John 11:41–42. Challenge students to write a prayer like His, containing confidence, purpose, and thanksgiving.
- Ask students to choose one of the events they listed in the "Out to Lunch" section and reconsider how God was involved in the event. Think of ways in which He may have been showing His love.

Lord, If You Had Been There ...

 Out to Lunch

Are there events or situations that make you think God is "out to lunch" and not watching what's going on in the world? Give an example.

 Taking God Seriously

How does it feel to deeply love and care for people who don't understand your way of loving? Read **John 11:1–45**.

- How do you think Martha and Mary felt when Jesus did not respond immediately to their urgent distress call?

- Why was Jesus so troubled by the two grieving sisters and their sympathizers?

- What was Jesus' strategy for dealing with Martha and Mary's crisis? Did it work?

> *From one man He made every nation of men, that they should inhabit the whole earth; and He determined the times set for them and the exact places where they should live. God did this so that men would seek Him and perhaps reach out for Him and find Him, though He is not far from each one of us.*
> *Acts 17:26–27*

Here Today—Here Tomorrow!

What is really happening when we don't recognize or understand Jesus' response to our distress calls? See what special insight and reassurance **Acts 18:9–10** offers.

- Which "special agents" has God provided to guide, encourage, and protect you as a disciple of Jesus Christ? Make a list.

- Whom are you guiding, encouraging, and protecting as a "special agent" of God? Make a list.

25 Loving Enemies?

Luke 6:27–38 (OLIC: February 18, 2001)

Purpose

With God's help, we can break down walls of hate and grow in our love for others—even enemies—because of the forgiveness we have in Jesus Christ.

Opening (10 minutes). Using a collection of straws, tape, old newspapers, and string, have two teams of students each build a "fortress" wall. After five minutes of "building," give an inflated balloon to each team and allow them two minutes to try to knock down the opposing team's wall using only the balloon! Ask:

- "What are some 'walls' people build—both physical and emotional—to protect or insulate themselves from others?" (Prejudices, cliques, attitudes, body language.)
- "Why do people put up walls?"
- "How can building walls create enemies?"

1. Characteristics of an Enemy (15 minutes). Distribute copies of the student page. Invite students to respond to the first question. You may want to help students by suggesting that they think of some of the traits and characteristics of "bad guys" from history, movies, TV, or stories. Invite volunteers to share examples of "enemy characteristics" with the group. Give the class time to complete the remaining questions and share their answers with the group.

2. The Word (20 minutes). Read aloud or have volunteers read aloud Luke 6:27–38. Invite student responses to the first question in this section. Point out that Jesus' teaching is very different from our accustomed view of the world. It makes us feel upside down and inside out. We have to face His words head on if we are ever to make any sense out of them. It would be easier if Jesus had said, "Try to avoid your enemies" or "Don't hate your enemies." But the command to love—well, it just seems like too much. Have students share their responses to the next two questions in this section.

Point out that we can't take on an enemy wall by ourselves. Christ broke down the walls of sin and hate through His death for us on the cross. He brings us hope for life by His victory over death. Only in Christ and by the power of the Holy Spirit can we truly love our enemies.

Have students read Romans 12:17–21 and answer the two questions on the student page.

Explain that the expression "heap burning coals on his head" was used to convey the hope that after being treated with kindness, the enemy would see faith in God at work and repent of their sin.

3. What about My Enemies? (10 minutes). Invite volunteers to share their ideas for what they can do to break down the walls of hate, fear, and trouble. If your class is large, you may wish to allow students to process this in small groups.

Then ask students, alone or in pairs, to complete their action plan for tearing down an enemy wall with God's power.

Closing (5 minutes). Ask students to think of someone who is an enemy or who once was an enemy and with whom they are now reconciled. Invite students to pray silently for the person they identified. Lead the group in prayer, seeking God's healing in all our broken relationships and His power to break down the walls that divide people.

Extending the Lesson

- Ask students to share how they think Jesus' enemies reacted to His teaching.
- Suggest that students keep a prayer journal of walls that have been broken with the power of God's Spirit in the world and in their lives.

Loving Enemies?

1 Characteristics of an Enemy

What are the traits or characteristics of a person whom you had or have a difficult time dealing with or who has caused you trouble? Use initials or a fictitious name to describe the situation.

What made this person a potential "enemy"?

How did this person make you feel?

2 The Word

Read **Luke 6:27–38**.
What does Jesus say that we should do with enemies?

What response did Jesus have toward His enemies?

What was the hope that He had in dealing with those who hated Him?

Read **Romans 12:17–21**. What do you think might be the result of acting in kindness toward an enemy?

What do "burning coals" have to do with enemies?

3 What about My Enemies?

What can you do for enemies, or when you see your friends fighting, to break down the walls of hate, fear, and trouble?

Complete an action plan to break down an enemy wall:

Name	Time Frame	Plan of Action

26 Have You Been to the Mountain?

Luke 9:28–36; John 14:1–14 (OLIC: February 25, 2001)

Purpose

All young people may not have had a transforming "mountaintop" spiritual experience, but God is at work in their lives, by the Holy Spirit, to bring assurance and quiet strength for daily living.

Opening (10 minutes). Stop by a travel agency for some posters and brochures from some exciting exotic locations or obtain descriptions of locations and pictures from the Internet. Place the material around the room as students arrive.

Give your students five minutes to pick "the most exciting and wonderful vacation spot." After the students have picked their vacation spot, have them share with the group. Ask, "What makes that vacation spot unique and special? What makes a vacation a once-in-a-lifetime experience?"

1. Mountaintop Experiences (5 minutes). Distribute copies of the student handout. Ask students to complete the questions. You can prime the students' thinking by suggesting such things as a vacation or camp experience, a church service, their confirmation, a retreat, or a youth gathering. Invite students to share their responses with the group.

2. A Mountaintop Experience with God (20 minutes). Read Luke 9:28–36.

Have students complete the first question. Remind the students how important these great prophets of Israel were for the Jews. Point out the transformation that Jesus undergoes. Even after everything else the disciples had seen, this transfiguration was an amazing experience! The reality of Jesus' divine nature gave hope and power to the disciples.

Ask students to complete the next question and share their insights.

2. Face-to-Face with God (15 minutes). Read John 14:1–14. Point out that by the power of the Holy Spirit,

God reveals Himself to us today through His Word and Sacraments. Worship and Bible study can become mountaintop experiences where God fills our lives with the love of Christ, helps us grow in faith, and makes us more aware of the needs of people around us. Worshiping alone or with others, praying with a friend, helping others in a servant event, leading a vacation Bible school class, or even experiencing a crisis can find us face-to-face with God.

Invite students to discuss the questions on their handout with two or three other students.

Closing (10 minutes). Have students each cut out one picture of their favorite vacation spot from the brochures and posters you have provided. Glue these on a piece of poster board under the heading "Have You Been to the Mountain?" Leave one-third of the poster board empty under the heading "The Love of God Caught Me ..."

After students have glued their picture in place, pass the poster around the room and invite them to write a time when they experienced the love and trust of God. Close in quiet prayer, giving thanks and praise to God for transforming our hearts to hope and trust.

Extending the Lesson

- Read about God's transforming power in Exodus 3:1–10; 1 Kings 18:22–39; and Acts 9:1–6. What impact did the power of God have in each of these events?

- Have students prepare a survey for the congregation that asks people to tell about an event that has had a significant impact on their faith and to describe a place or event where they have known the power of God.

Have You Been to the Mountain?

1 Mountaintop Experiences

Tell about a time and place when you experienced a feeling of awe at the beauty of God's creation.

What was it that made a lasting impression on you (feelings, surroundings, etc.)?

2 A Mountaintop Experience with God

Read **Luke 9:28–36**.
A. Why was this an awe-filled experience for Peter, James, and John?

B. Why do you think Jesus wanted His disciples to see this event?

Especially look at the following phrases:

- "They spoke about His departure" (**verse 31**).

- "They saw His glory" (**verse 32**).

- "This is My Son, whom I have chosen; listen to Him" (**verse 35**).

3 Face-to-Face with God

Read **John 14:1–14**. What three phrases do you think were most comforting to the disciples in this reading?

How could these phrases be mountaintop experiences for people that you know today? Under what circumstances could these words be mountaintop experiences for people in our world?

What message is most comforting to you in these words from Jesus?

27 Who's My Neighbor?

Luke 10:25–37; Micah 6:8; Matthew 5:7; Luke 6:36 (OLIC: March 4, 2001)

Purpose

The word *neighbors* implies those who live nearby. Jesus has another definition. In this study, students will be led to discover a broader definition of *neighbors*—those who are touched by and touch others with God's mercy.

Opening (10 minutes). Ask your class, "Does anyone here have $5.00? I need a little extra for lunch after church." If they ask, tell them you are not planning on paying them back. Ask, "If someone you did not know came up to you and asked for a handout, what would you do?" Ask those to whom this has really happened to share their experiences.

1. The Issue (10 minutes). Distribute copies of the student page. Have a student read the quotation. Point out that many may feel this way. Ask, "Why do you think that they would make this statement? How would you respond?"

2. The Word (20 minutes). Group students in fours. Have each person in the group look up one of the Bible passages in this section. Then have them share answers within the group.

After they are done, ask, "What concept is common to all these passages?" (Mercy or some form of it.) Ask for a definition of *mercy*. According to the dictionary, mercy is being kind and compassionate in your treatment of another person. Have the students take turns reading Luke 10:25–37 verse by verse and discuss the questions on the student page. Make sure students realize that our "neighborly" ways are possible only because Jesus is our "neighbor." He showed mercy for us by dying for our sins and working in us through the Spirit to give us new life.

3. The World (15 minutes). Have the students read the situation on the student page to themselves. Ask, "What kind of problem could come up at three in the morning?" Let volunteers share responses to the question "Whom would you call?" Point out that God loves them and will provide help in direct and indirect ways—through events and through caring people.

Ask the students to think about someone in their school, neighborhood, or family who needs help in some way right now—a person they could assist this week. Allow students time to think through and write down some ways they could help.

Closing (5 minutes). Close with a prayer that God would help the students reach out in mercy to the people who need help and that He would encourage them to do so daily.

Extending the Lesson

- Have the students commit to reporting about the person they needed to show mercy to and how they felt.
- Plan a class outing to extend a hand of mercy to someone in your community.

Who's My Neighbor?

1 The Issue

"Religious people are supposed to act a certain way, right? I mean, they're supposed to help the poor, get involved with community events, help their neighbors, and stuff. If I can't expect help from a person who goes to church, whom can I expect it from?" Do you agree? How would you respond?

2 The Word

Review these four passages.
Look for God's plan for you.

Luke 10:36–37

Micah 6:8

Matthew 5:7

Luke 6:36
How is the message in each
of these passages consistent?

Read **Luke 10:25–37**.
What is God calling His people to do?

How is that possible?

3 The World

It's 3:00 A.M. and you have a problem … a big one. Whom could you call? It would have to be someone you could trust, who would be there for you with both their head and their heart.

Whom would you call? Why?

Whom do you know right now who is hurting and may have no one to call on for assistance? Can you be the merciful one in that person's life?

Take time to develop a simple plan to make yourself available to this person to share God's mercy in helpful ways.

28 Building Up Your Strength

Luke 22:7–38; Mark 9:24; John 6:37; 1 John 1:7 (OLIC: March 11, 2001)

Purpose

Communion is a sacrament given to us by Jesus Christ for the strengthening of our faith. By the grace of God, the students will see Communion as a way God builds strong faith in their lives.

Opening (10 minutes). Ask, "If you could take something that would make you stronger, smarter, or more attractive, would you do it? Why or why not? Do you know anything like that? Today we will explore how the Lord's Supper can make our faith stronger."

1. The Issue (10 minutes). Distribute copies of the student page. Have students check all the things they think or feel when they take Communion. Invite volunteers to share their responses, explaining why they chose the words they did.

2. The Word (20 minutes). As you read Luke 22:7–38, have the students follow along and underline words that indicate power or strength for them. Discuss students' choices.

In groups, have students look up the other three passages. Have each group write what the passage says about making their faith strong.

3. The World (10 minutes). Encourage the students to thoughtfully write an ending to the sentences. Allow volunteers to share answers. Reflect on what it is that God has given us in the Lord's Supper to keep our faith strong.

Closing (5 minutes). Have the students stand in a circle and, if they are willing, hold hands. Pray, or let the students pray, offering thanks to God for providing the Lord's Supper as a gift that strengthens our faith. Ask God to strengthen each of you the next time you share in His Holy Meal together.

Extending the Lesson

- Review the sections about Communion in *Luther's Small Catechism with Explanation*. Read either Luther's questions and answers or questions 296–304.
- Have students interview members of the congregation, asking them why or how the Lord's Supper strengthens their faith. Or have your class members interview students preparing for their first Communion, asking why they are looking forward to participating in the Sacrament. Use a video camera, if appropriate, to record answers.

Building Up Your Strength

The Issue

What do you feel or think when you attend the Lord's Supper?

Joy

Fear

Love

Closeness to God

Solemnity

Sadness

Strength

Power

Wonder

Commitment

_____

_____

The Word

Jesus institutes (that is, celebrates for the first time) the Sacrament of Communion in **Luke 22:7–38.** Read the passage, underlining the words that indicate power or strength for you.

What do the following have to say about making your faith strong?

Mark 9:24

John 6:37

1 John 1:7

The World

I am weak spiritually …

The Lord's Supper gives me strength …

My faith is made strong …

29 Earning Our Trust

Luke 22:39–46 (OLIC: March 18, 2001)

Purpose

Teens will discover for themselves that although human relationships are important to us, Christ alone is worthy of all our trust. Even though we let Him down, He never lets us down.

Opening (10 minutes). Ask for three volunteers. One student will be blindfolded and asked to walk through some obstacles. Take the other two students aside. Tell one to lead the blindfolded person through the obstacles by calling out bad directions. The second person is supposed to lead the person through the obstacles by calling out good directions. The remaining students will stand around the classroom as obstacles. When everyone is ready, tell the blindfolded person it's okay to listen to either person giving directions. The blindfolded person will quickly realize who is trustworthy and who is not. At the end, ask, "How did you learn which person could be trusted?"

1. Trust Me (10 minutes). Distribute copies of the student page. Ask students to discuss the questions in the first section in small groups. After a few minutes, ask, "What makes people trustworthy? Is it what they say, or is it what they do? If you have a friend who continually lets you down, what is holding that friendship together? Do you trust that person? Do you rely on that person? Who in your life has proven to be the most reliable person?"

2. Digging Deeper (10 minutes). Ask the students to read Luke 22:39–46. Discuss question 1 on the student page. As students think about their different temptations, set the scene of what has been happening. "It's late at night. The disciples have had the holiday meal, and they know that Jesus is praying nearby." Give students time to be creative as they consider what they would have done. Ask, "How can prayer help when we are tempted?"

Discuss questions 2–4 on the student page. Lead students to understand that Jesus followed the Father's will in order to accomplish our salvation.

3. Whom Do You Trust? (15 minutes). How would students describe Jesus in this passage? Say, "This story gives us a good picture of how human Jesus really was. Can you relate to His suffering? Do you think Jesus knows how it feels to be let down by friends?" Have students fill out the table on the student sheet. Ask them what they have learned about trusting their friends, their parents, and Jesus. Look up Matthew 26:41. Jesus knows exactly what it is like to be human. Because we are weak, He was strong. He obeyed His Father's will perfectly when we would have failed. Because of Jesus, we have the promise of eternal life. We know that we can count on Jesus now as well.

Closing (5 minutes). Read Romans 15:13. Point out that when we put our trust in Jesus, we are filled with joy and peace because He does not let us down. Through faith in Him, hope overflows from us so that all the world may see the power of the Holy Spirit at work in our lives. Close with a short prayer.

Extending the Lesson.

- Have your students look up John 14:1. Ask, "What does this tell us about our relationship with Christ now?"

Earning Our Trust

1 Trust Me

1. Have you ever been let down by a friend?

2. What happens to your trust of a person who lets you down?

3. Has a friend ever come through for you when you didn't expect it?

2 Digging Deeper

Read **Luke 22:39–46.**

1. What is the first thing Jesus tells His disciples to do? Why? What temptations could they have?

2. In **verse 42**, does Jesus know what He has to do? Does He want to do it?

3. Is it more important for Jesus to do His will or the Father's will? Why?

4. What did Jesus do when He found the disciples asleep?

3 Whom Do You Trust?

Put a check in the column if you can trust the person in the situation given.

We trust someone because they always ...	Friends	Parents	Jesus
keep their promises to us.			
help us when we are in trouble.			
have been faithful in the past.			
do what is best for us (not just what we want).			
put us above themselves.			
sacrifice for us.			

30 What Makes a Great Christian?

Luke 22:24–35, 54–62 (OLIC: March 25, 2001)

Purpose

We cannot be truly great in the kingdom of God until we have faith in Jesus and His promise of forgiveness rather than our own actions.

Opening (10 minutes). Pass out index cards and have the students write down one thing they are afraid of. Gather the cards and ask volunteers to act out some of the fears listed for the rest of the group to guess. After each pantomime, ask how many are afraid of that thing. Tell the students it is easy to be brave until you have to actually confront your fears.

1. Great in the Kingdom (10 minutes). Distribute copies of the student page. Have the students complete the first section. Read through each of the items listed and ask students to indicate the items they circled. Ask what other things they listed. All these are fine things, but in the kingdom of God, it is not what we do that makes us great in the eyes of God.

2. Digging Deeper (15 minutes). Tell the students to turn to Luke 22:24–30 and read it aloud. Discuss the first two questions. Ask, "What makes a person humble? What gives a person a servant heart? Do you think the disciples had servant hearts at this point?" Read verses 31–34 and discuss question 3. Then turn to Luke 22:54–62 and discuss questions 4–6. Ask, "Do you think Peter changed his mind about following Christ to prison or death? What caused Peter to change his mind? Fear took over and Peter couldn't follow through on his promise to Jesus. How far would you go to defend Jesus? How is that different than Peter?"

3. Would You Rather ... ? (10 minutes). Have the students mark their choice on the student sheets and go through the items one at a time. Discuss Luke 22:32. Ask, "What was Peter supposed to do? What does that mean? What makes Peter able to do this? What makes us great in the kingdom of God? It is important to be a servant, but it is when we recognize our sinfulness and are healed by Christ's forgiveness that we are the best servants of all. That is why confession and absolution are so important in our worship life. If we draw our strength from Jesus' forgiveness, we have the power to do anything God wants us to do. Only through Christ can we serve God with all of our heart. In Him we are great in the kingdom of God."

Closing (5 minutes). Close by having students break into small groups and write a confession of sins together. Have each group read their confession and then remind them that all their sins are forgiven because of Jesus' suffering, death, and resurrection.

Extending the Lesson

• Have students read the story of the prodigal in Luke 15:11–32. What parallels can we draw between this parable and the life of Matthew?

WHAT MAKES A GREAT CHRISTIAN?

1
Great in the Kingdom

Circle the things that make you stand out as a Christian:

Read the Bible

Memorize the Ten Commandments

Serve as president of the youth group

Lead a Bible study at school

Be a nursery attendant at church

Volunteer in the church office

Usher

Other _____

_____

2
Digging Deeper

Read **Luke 22:24–34, 54–62**.

1. What were the disciples arguing about? What criteria do you think they used?

2. According to Jesus, what makes someone great in the kingdom of God?

3. Do you think Peter thought of himself as a great disciple? On whose strength was he relying when he boasted in verse 33?

4. What was Peter afraid of when he was sitting in the courtyard? What did his fear cause him to do?

5. After Peter denied Christ, what did Jesus do? What do you think Jesus was thinking?

6. Why did Peter weep bitterly when he looked into the eyes of Christ?

3

Would You Rather ... ?

have boastful friends . . . . .or . . . . have humble friends?

be condemned . . . . .or. . . . . be forgiven?

know someone who has struggles in life . .or . . . . know someone who is "perfect"?

have a friend who likes you a lot . . . . .or . . . . have a friend who likes himself or herself a lot?

listen to someone talk . . . . .or . . . . talk to someone who listens?

31 Stop the Violence

Luke 22:66–23:25 (OLIC: April 1, 2001)

Purpose

Young people hear about and experience forms of violence on a daily basis. Jesus' action and forgiveness provide an alternative, non-violent response.

1. Word Power (15 minutes). Distribute copies of the student page. Have students read the directions and complete section 1. Tell them the words can go in more than one box. When they have completed the chart, discuss students' reasons for choosing to put a word in a certain box.

2. Into the Word (20 minutes). As a group read Luke 23:1–25. Have students work in pairs to complete the activity. Discuss why they chose to put verses where they did. Point out the vast difference in power that Jesus uses as compared to His accusers. This Gospel action reveals that love is a greater power than violence.

3. Your Power (5 minutes). Ask students to review Luke 23:12 and discuss the question concerning the power that Pilate and Herod shared. (These former enemies became friends when Pilate deferred to Herod on the matter of Jesus.) Continue with a discussion of questions 2 and 3. Sadly, we have to admit that because of our sinful nature, we are not much different than the crowds who were violently screaming for Jesus to be crucified. How different from Jesus' response to us, as He forgives us and makes us His children through the victory that He won on the cross.

Closing (5 minutes). (You will need a bowl of water, ground pepper, and a small amount of liquid detergent.) Take a bowl of clean water (representing the world) and have all gather closely around the bowl. Shake the pepper (representing violent powers) on top of the water. Dip one finger in liquid detergent (to represent Jesus' forgiving love) and touch the water in the bowl. The "powers" quickly move to the very edges of the bowl. The power of Jesus' love is that strong in the world. Close in prayer, asking God to help us share Christ's love in the world around us.

Extending the Lesson

• Ask your students, "What television shows or movies have you recently seen that have more violence than you initially realized? Many people only look for physical violence. What more subtle forms of violence does the media reveal? How can Christians respond?"

68

Stop the Violence

1 Word Power

Write each of the following words in at least one box below to identify the type of power with which it is connected.

abuse	guilt	punishment
anger	hate	revenge
corporate	humiliation	ridicule
cruelty	jealousy	secrecy
domination	love	silence
economic	lying	truth
facts and numbers	oppression	words
fear	prominence	yelling
forgiveness	of position	

Physical Power

Emotional or Psychological Power

Natural Power

Beneficial Power

Dangerous Power

Implied Power

Subtle or Hidden Power

Violent Power

2 Into the Word

Read **Luke 23:1–25**. Write the verse numbers in the boxes in section 1 to describe the power that you think may be occurring within a verse.

3 Your Power

1. **Verse 12** indicates that Pilate and Herod became friends that day. Why might this have happened? How might this be explained in terms of the powers they each had?

2. Review **verses 14–22.** Why do you think Pilate and the crowd responded to Jesus with violence? In what ways are we like them?

3. Jesus turned defeat into victory. He allowed Himself to be humiliated, crucified, and put to death out of love for all people, even those who acted violently toward Him. How can His victory—His payment for our sin and His resurrection—be power for when people are tempted to act violently and experience violence?

32 The Cross Is the Thing

Luke 23:26–56 (Luke 19:28–44) (OLIC: April 8, 2001)

Purpose

Your students see crosses everywhere. But they may not often have a chance to think through what the cross means—and what it means to them. In this session, they look again at the death of Jesus and what that death on the cross means in their lives.

Opening (10 minutes). Draw a swastika on the board or on a piece of paper. Show it to the class. What does this "cross" mean? What would you think if you saw this symbol on a building? on a person's arm? How would you react? Why has it come to represent hatred and violence?

1. Crosses (10 minutes). Distribute copies of the student page. Give students time to describe (or draw) a cross they like. Discuss the text. Encourage them to talk about what crosses mean in our current culture. Ask, "How can wearing a cross be a positive witness of faith? How might it be negative? For some the cross is a statement of faith; for others it is just an ornament. How can the meaning of the cross be damaged by some who wear it for the wrong reason?"

2. Into the Word (20 minutes). Read the Palm Sunday account in Luke 19:28–44 to set the scene. Ask, "What did the people expect of Jesus?" (He would lead a revolution against the Romans.) "What kind of a Savior did they think Jesus would be?" (They were looking for a political leader.) "How might they have shown their disappointment when He did not lead the revolution they had hoped for?" (They denied and betrayed Him.)

Read the story of the crucifixion of Jesus from Luke 23:26–56 aloud. You may want to assign various parts for a dramatic reading. Parts may include a narrator, Jesus, the crowd, the soldiers, two criminals, and the army officer.

After reading the account, lead the class in a discussion about what they heard. Ask, "What is surprising about this story?" (Answers will vary.) "What is fearful or frightening?" (The anger and hatred toward Jesus.) "What in it reminds you of the swastika?" (Expressions of hate and death.) "What do you think Jesus' death on the cross meant to the people there? to the crowds?" (Death of another prophet.) "to the soldiers?" (Some mocked, others believed.) "to his followers?" (Lost and confused.) "Why do you think it took until Easter for the disciples to understand the death of Jesus?" (They didn't yet understand the fact that Jesus would rise again.)

3. Bringing It Home (10 minutes). Read together Ephesians 2:8 and Philippians 2:8–11. Ask, "What does Paul say is the meaning of the cross? What is the message of salvation for us?" Then direct students to write an answer to the question on the student sheet. Ask those who are willing to share their statements. Talk about how students could share their confession about the meaning of the cross with others at home, in school, and with friends.

Closing (5 minutes). Sing or read together a hymn like "Lift High the Cross" (*Lutheran Worship*, 311). Ask students to offer prayers asking the Spirit to keep the true meaning of the cross in our hearts.

Extending the Lesson

• Make or purchase simple wooden or metal crosses for each of the students. Ask them to carry the cross this week and to think about it when they touch it or see it. They might report their experiences next week.

• Ask students to wear or display a cross this week (on their notebooks, for example). At your next session, talk about the reactions to that cross.

The Cross Is the Thing

 **Crosses**

- Describe or draw your favorite cross. Why is it your favorite?

- Lots of people wear crosses—pastors wear them, some men and women wear them as earrings, some even have cross tattoos. What do you think the cross means to those wearers?

2 Into the Word

Read **Luke 19:28–44.** What kind of Messiah did people expect?

Read **Luke 23:26–56.** What kind of Messiah did Jesus prove Himself to be?

3 Bringing It Home

Read **Ephesians 2:8** and **Philippians 2:8–11.**
What does the cross mean to you?

33 More Than Easter

Luke 24:1–11; Matthew 28:1–10; 1 Corinthians 15:1–11 (OLIC: April 15, 2001)

Purpose

Students will be familiar with Easter and its trappings. In this lesson they review the real meaning of Easter and consider what the resurrection of Jesus means to them.

Opening (10 minutes). Write the words *peace, love,* and *hope* on the board or on a piece of paper. Ask, "Which do you think is easiest to find: real peace, real love, or real hope? Why? Why are each of these difficult to find? How do people look for them in the wrong places? What can happen to people who 'have no hope'?"

Easter and More (10 minutes). Bring some Easter things—flowers, colorful eggs, and butterfly pictures—to class. Or ask students to draw or describe some of the things we normally associate with Easter on their copy of the student page. Discuss: "What does this stuff mean? What do you think it means out in the world? What does it say to you? What do these things have to do with resurrection?"

2. Into the Word (20 minutes). Ask students to work together to recall and tell the real Easter story. They might work in pairs and write down the details they remember. After a few minutes, invite volunteers to share their work.

Read aloud, or have volunteers read aloud, Luke 24:1–11 and Matthew 28:1–10. Compare the accounts with what the students recalled, listing the things that happened.

Ask, "What do you think that first Easter meant to the women? to the disciples? When do you think they really understood what happened on that morning?"

Have students read 1 Corinthians 15:1–11 and answer the questions on the student page. After allowing them to work for a while, bring the group together to share and discuss their answers.

3. Bringing It Home (10 minutes). Ask students to respond to the question on the student page. Ask volunteers to read what they have written.

Discuss what the resurrection of Jesus has to do with
- His death;
- the death of our loved ones;
- our own death;
- our hope of new life.

Invite the students to look again at the Easter items that you brought or that they drew. Ask, "How can these symbols of Easter bring to mind the real story and meaning of Easter? How can they help us remember and tell the story of the resurrection?"

Closing (5 minutes). Sing together an Easter hymn. Ask a volunteer to offer a prayer asking the Spirit to renew the students' hope in the resurrection.

Extending the Lesson

- Suggest the students carry and give away simple Easter objects (flowers, chocolate rabbits, colored eggs) this week. As they give, they might share the Easter story. Talk about their experience at your next session.
- Ask students to write a letter of hope to someone who is grieving or lonely. They might write the letter to themselves to save to read when they feel lost and lonely. Those who are willing might share their letters.

MORE THAN EASTER

1 Easter and More

Draw some of the symbols of Easter.

What do these things have to do with the Easter resurrection of Jesus?

2 Into the Word

What specific details do you remember about the first Easter? Who visited the tomb? In what order? How did they react? Why? (Check out **Luke 24:1–11** if you need help.)

Read **1 Corinthians 15:1–11.**
What does Paul tell us is the meaning of that first Easter?

What does it mean about our own death?

What can we hope for?

3 Bringing It Home

What does Easter mean to you?

34 Miraculous Fishing and Love

John 21:1–25 (OLIC: April 22, 2001)

Purpose

In this session the students will know that God provides for them in miraculous ways, especially when it comes to their salvation.

Opening (5 minutes). Ask students to talk about their most memorable fishing trip (if any). Did they catch any fish? Did the big one get away? Talk about the different kinds of fishing (deep sea fishing, fly fishing, lake fishing) they may have experienced.

1. Thinking about Miracles (15 minutes). Distribute copies of the student page. Challenge students to think about the different miracles in the Old and New Testaments. Have students record which Bible miracle they think was the most spectacular. Discuss the students' choices. Why did they select the miracle that they did? The most miraculous thing that affects us personally is that despite the fact that we are sinful and unfaithful, God still loves us (see Romans 5:6–8).

2. The Miracles in John 21 (20 minutes). Ask volunteers to read John 21:1–25 aloud. Or have the students read it as a drama.

Ask the students to identify the two major miracles that occurred in this lesson (the miraculous catch of fish, the miraculous love shown to Peter).

Ask a student to reread verses 15–17. Then challenge the students to honestly answer the next question. You might start by suggesting that your actions certainly don't always show Him that you love Him all the time.

Get students thinking about God's miraculous love. St. Paul reminds us that "while we were still sinners, Christ died for us" (Romans 5:8). He loves you despite the things you think, say, or do. Your salvation is sure (Ephesians 2:8–9).

3. Sharing the Miracles (10 minutes). Remind the students that God performs some of His miraculous deeds through us. Ask the students to identify the clear command God gives to Peter and to us ("feed My lambs"). Let the students list some specific things they can do this week to carry out this command. Discuss these ways. Encourage them to add additional things to their list as they share in class.

Closing (5 minutes). Invite the students to join in prayer, thanking God for His constant love for them and asking for power to carry out the command of sharing that love with others. Encourage them to pray specifically for help to do the things they have listed on their worksheets.

Extending the Lesson

- Ask the students to interview a full-time church worker. They can ask, "Why did you decide on this profession? What are the joys and sorrows of church work?" These interviews could be shared at the next class.

- Ask the students to jot a note or card to someone they know who has a special need to hear of God's love. Encourage them to specifically tell of God's love shown in the sending of His Son, Jesus Christ, to redeem that person for eternity.

Miraculous Fishing and Love

Thinking about Miracles

The most spectacular miracle in the Bible was the time when …

Sharing the Miracles

What clear command does Jesus give to Peter—and to each of us—in **verses 15–17**?

List some specific things we can do this week to carry out this command.

The Miracles in John 21

Identify the two miracles in **John 21:1–20.**

Read **John 21:15–17.** Suppose Jesus asked you the same question He asked Peter. How would you answer?

- A.   Of course I love You, Lord. All the time.
- B.   Well, once in a while.
- C.   I try to love You, but I know I don't always.
- D.   Never.

What is miraculous about God's love?

1. **Romans 5:8** _____

   _____ .

2. **Ephesians 2:8–9** _____

   _____ .

35 I Love You, Man!

Acts 9:1–20 (OLIC: April 29, 2001)

Purpose

In this session the students will be reassured that God loves people. Surprising as it may seem, He loves even those who fight against Him and are His enemies.

1. Surprise (5 minutes). Distribute copies of the student page. Ask the students to comment on the surprises listed in the first section. Have them describe the biggest surprise they've ever experienced.

2. The Surprises in Acts 9 (20 minutes). Ask volunteers to read Acts 9:1–20 aloud. Or allow students to read it as a drama. Ask the students to identify the major surprises in these verses.

Surprise, Ananias! Ask the students how they would have reacted to Jesus' request of Ananias. Ananias addresses Saul as "Brother Saul" (Acts 9:17). Inquire how many of the students find it that easy to forgive an enemy and call him a "brother." It is the Holy Spirit working within us that makes us able to forgive and love one another.

Surprise, people! Ask the students to read aloud Romans 5:6–11. Why is God's love for His people truly the biggest surprise that has ever occurred or will ever occur in history?

Surprise! Ask the students to think of what surprises they might have when they're in heaven someday. Think about how surprised some of those who were killed by Saul for their belief will be to see Saul (Paul) in heaven.

3. Sharing God's Surprises with Others (10 minutes). Review again in your own words the work of Ananias in the story. Ask the students if they can name any Ananiases in their life. Encourage them to talk specifically of how these people helped them grow in their faith.

Ask the students to reflect on those people who need to have an Ananias in their life. God has given each of us a purpose. It is to "make disciples" (Matthew 28:19). Encourage the students to give suggestions on how they might be an Ananias to these people.

Closing (5 minutes). Close by summarizing the surprise of God's love for His people. Ask the students to join you in singing "Jesus Loves Me, This I Know." Then ask the students to join hands and give thanks for the many surprises they've had in their lives—including God's love and salvation.

Extending the Lesson

- Have the students write a testimony of their faith and belief in Jesus Christ, mentioning specifically why faith is such a surprise. Encourage the students to share their testimonies at the next class.
- Have the students write a letter to their pastor, DCE, or youth leader thanking that person for helping them to walk with the Lord.

I Love You, Man!

1 Surprise!

Surprises come in unexpected packages and at unexpected times. How would these surprises make you feel?

A. "That wasn't hamburger you ate. It was Alpo pet food!"

B. "Mom, someone from Sweepstakes Clearing House would like to talk to you."

C. "Dad, I think there is a large snake in our toilet bowl."

D. "Congratulations, it looks like you're going to have triplets."

What is the biggest surprise you think you've ever had?

2 The Surprises in Acts 9

The major surprises in Acts 9:1–20 include

"Surprise, Ananias!" How did Ananias react to God's request? **(Acts 9:17)**

"Surprise, people!" In what way is God's love for His people the biggest surprise that has ever occurred or will ever occur? **(Romans 5:6–11)**

"Surprise!" What kind of surprises do you think you'll experience in heaven?

3 Sharing God's Surprises with Others

Who has been or is an Ananias in your life?

Do you know of someone who needs an Ananias in his or her life? Who and why?

36 Being Bold

Acts 9:20–31; 13:1–33 (OLIC: May 6, 2001)

Purpose

Young people have many opportunities to tell of Christ's love to the people around them. The aim of this lesson is to help them see opportunities to be bold witnesses for God and His church.

Opening (5 minutes). Ask the group to brainstorm ways people reveal they are Christians. Have a recorder write the examples on a chalkboard or newsprint. You may want to get the group started by giving examples.

1. Showing the Faith (10 minutes). Distribute copies of the student page. Allow the students time to fill in their personal responses. Ask volunteers to share specific ways and times they let others see their faith.

Ask, "Is it always easy to show yourself as a Christian?" Discuss student answers, acknowledging difficulties and reminding them of the powerful help provided by the Holy Spirit.

2. Studying the Word (10 minutes). In pairs or small groups have the students read the passages and work through the questions. To avoid confusion, remind them that Saul's name was later changed to Paul.

When you bring the group back together, ask for responses to the first set of questions on the student page. Reinforce the idea that Paul's ministry was at times very difficult, yet God moved him to continue.

Reread Acts 13:16 to the group. Ask, "Whom is Paul talking to?" (Primarily the Jews.) "Why does he recount their history?" (He starts with what they already know. Then he takes the opportunity to build on that.)

3. Sharing the Gospel (20 minutes). Remind the students that Paul, led by the Holy Spirit, chose his words carefully as he witnessed to people. The Holy Spirit empowers us to do the same. We probably would not witness about Christ to everyone in exactly the same way. God helps us to pick appropriate approaches and times.

Work through the examples on the student page one at a time. Reinforce the fact that not all witnessing opportunities and approaches are identical.

Then ask the students, "What one thing stays the same in all these situations?" (We proclaim that we are saved by grace through Christ's death and resurrection.)

Read and discuss Matthew 28:19. God's command that we make disciples of all people is possible only by the power of the Holy Spirit.

Closing (5 minutes). Ask students to once again think of ways they can show, in their speech and actions, that they are Christians. After allowing a silent minute or two for this, ask them to silently think of times this week when they will be able to put those ideas into action. Reread Matthew 28:19 to the group and close in prayer.

Extending the Lesson

- Have students role-play the situations presented in section 3.
- Ask students to make a list this week of the specific ways they see people showing and sharing their faith. Share these next week.

Being Bold

1 Showing the Faith

We see and hear the faith of God's people in many ways. How do *your* actions show *your* faith?

When might you be given opportunities to show your faith? List some specific examples:

2 Studying the Word

Read **Acts 9:20–31** and **Acts 13:1–12.**

* What problems did Saul (Paul) face in his ministry? Why can telling about God be difficult? What can make it easier? How was Paul's ministry blessed?

* Read **Acts 13:13–33.** Whom is Paul talking to? Why does he recount their history?

3  Sharing the Gospel

How might you witness to

- a little child?

- a very sick elderly neighbor?

- a non-Christian friend from school?

- a friend whose faith seems weak?

- a person who tries to convert you to a non-Christian religion?

What one thing stays the same in all these situations?

What is God's command to us in **Matthew 28:19?** How can we possibly do that?

37 Know It—Show It

Acts 13:44–52; 16:1–5; 2 Timothy 1:5–7; 3:14–16 (OLIC: May 13, 2001)

Purpose
This lesson will help students identify how God has given them knowledge of Jesus their Savior and His will for their lives. It will help them see how they can share that faith and love with others.

Opening (5 minutes). Play this game with the students: For each statement, students should quickly stand up if it applies to them, then immediately sit down again. Read the list rapidly to keep the game fast paced. Add some of your own examples. (Outrageous ones can be fun!)

Stand up if you know ...
- how to read.
- how to fly a plane.
- how to play volleyball.
- how to jump on one foot.
- the name of the vice-president of the United States.
- how to play the piano.
- your grandmother's middle name.
- (Add your own.)
- that God loves you.

1. How Do I Know? (5 minutes). Distribute copies of the student page. Ask students how they know that God loves them. Allow time for discussion. Let the students individually work through the list of ways God teaches about His love. Students and teacher can share answers with the group.

2. A Look to the Word (15 minutes). Have volunteers read aloud the passages listed on the student page. Discuss the questions and have students fill in the answers as you go. Ask, "Why was the work of Paul, Barnabas, and Timothy so important?" (These men were sharing their faith with many other people.) "How might Timothy's life have been different if his mother and grandmother had not shared their faith with him? How would your life be different if you had not been given opportunities to learn about God?"

3. Whom Can I Tell? (20 minutes). Direct the students to the last part of their page. It's very easy to think of people we *should* tell about Jesus. It's much more complex to actually plan for and then *do* it. Before the students begin to write, remind them that the Holy Spirit blesses their words and actions with His strength and power. He wants us to share the message of God's love. Our words will be full of His power, even though we may not see immediate results.

Direct the students to write down their plan. Those who are willing may share with the group. Those who are frustrated may appreciate the help the group might provide.

Closing (5 minutes). Have students begin by praying silently for the person or people with whom they intend to share God's Word. Then pray aloud to finish: "We thank You, God, for the power of Your Holy Spirit. Bless us as we share the wonderful news of Your love. Amen."

Extending the Lesson
- Have students write a thank-you letter to someone who has encouraged them in their faith.
- Encourage students to carry out their plan in section 3. Ask them to keep a journal including both prayers for the person and reactions to their efforts.

Know It—Show It

1 How Do I Know?

How do you know that God loves you? What or whom has He used to let you know about His love? Circle those that apply. Then add your own on the lines below.

The Bible

My parents _____

My friends _____

My pastor _____

_____

2 A Look to the Word

Read **Acts 13:44–52**. What were Paul and Barnabas doing?

Read **Acts 16:1–5**. Who joined them? What happened to the churches they visited? (**v. 5**)

Read **2 Timothy 1:5–7**. Who shared their faith with Timothy? Why did they do that?

Read **2 Timothy 3:14–16**. What is Paul's charge to Timothy? What does this passage mean for you?

3 Whom Can I Tell?

You are blessed to know about God's love for you and your sure hope of salvation. With whom can you share the Gospel? Think carefully about opportunities you may have.

My Plan: I will share the Good News of God's saving love:

Who? _____

_____

When? _____

_____

Where? _____

_____

Why? _____

_____

38 He's Talking, Are You Listening?

Acts 14:8–23; 16:6–15 (OLIC: May 20, 2001)

Purpose

Young people need reassurance that God does indeed speak to them today through His Word. As your students grow in their faith, they will listen for His voice and seek His guidance in their lives.

Opening (5 minutes). Play "Hot/Cold." While a volunteer leaves the room, hide an object and assign one student to direct the volunteer to the hidden object by saying "hot" or "cold." Tell the remaining students to distract the volunteer by saying words other than hot and cold or using hand motions. Discuss how the directions were more difficult to follow with all the distractions.

1. Who, Me? (5 minutes). Help students see that every day they make decisions how to act, where to go, what to say. Daily life is full of decisions, big and little. Sometimes we may wonder: Why doesn't God just tell me what He wants me to do? The truth: God has revealed His will to His people.

2. God Spoke (10 minutes). Have students circle their choices on the student page. Use the verses to guide a brief discussion on ways God speaks or has spoken to His people: dreams (Genesis 28:10–19), visions (Genesis 15:1), prophets (Hebrews 1:1), a whisper (1 Kings 19:12–13), Jesus (John 4:25–26), and the Holy Spirit (John 14:26).

3. Following Directions (10 minutes). Have students read Acts 16:6–15 and answer the question on the student page. God used the Holy Spirit and a vision to direct Paul where to go. God used circumstances to bring the Good News of Jesus Christ to Lydia and her household. It was not mere coincidence that she met Paul that day by the river, but a result of God's plan and timing.

4. How Does God Speak to People Today? (10 minutes). Have volunteers read each of the verses on the student page. As each verse is read, have students note the means by which God directs His people. Lead students to see the importance of being involved in a regular study of God's Word. The Word is the means by which God speaks to them today. Ask, "What do you think is the most important message God sends us through His Word?" Allow volunteers to respond and probe for the biblical source of each suggestion. If it is mentioned, invite students to consider John 20:31: "But these are written that you may believe … [and] have life." Have students share issues in their lives that require God's guidance. How does God's Word address those needs? What role do Christian friends or adult leaders play in seeking guidance?

Closing (5 minutes). As we seek God's guidance, He invites us to come to Him in prayer. Close in prayer, thanking God for His guidance in our lives.

Extending the Lesson

Pose the following questions to the group:
- Some friends say to you, "You're a Christian, right? Well, how do you know what God wants you to do?" You tell them …
- You hear a man on TV saying, "God told me He wanted me to start this new church." Do you think God really "spoke" to this man?

He's Talking. Are You Listening?

1 Who, Me?

What's the biggest decision you've had to make so far? Did you try to seek God's direction when you made that decision? How?

2 God Spoke

Circle all the ways you think God used to speak to His people in the Bible.

- Dreams
- Visions
- Prophets
- A whisper
- Jesus
- The Holy Spirit

3 Following Directions

Read **Acts 16:6–15**. How did God speak to Paul and his companions?

4 How Does God Speak to People Today?

- **Hebrews 1:1–2**

- **Luke 24:27**

- **John 14:26**

- **John 16:13–14**

- **2 Timothy 3:16–17**

Share a particular issue for which you or students your age need God's guidance.

39 Fearless Faith

Acts 16:16–40 (OLIC: May 27, 2001)

Purpose

It can be risky for young people to share their faith in Christ, let alone defend it. This lesson reminds us that God promises to strengthen our faith and support us as we have opportunities to share His message and love with others.

1. Have You Ever? (5 minutes). Use the checklist on the student page to discuss students' attempts to share their faith. Do students have a lack of opportunities to share their faith? Or do they avoid opportunities that arise? Explore with students what fears hinder them from sharing their faith.

2. Real-Life Faith Challenges (15 minutes). Discuss with students the real-life examples described. If possible, be prepared to share recent examples of young Christians who have met opposition to their faith.

3. Paul's Struggles (15 minutes). Have students work alone or with partners to complete this section. Have pairs share their insights with the whole group. Paul was trying to go to the place of prayer (verse 16). Despite Paul's struggles, God used Paul to share Jesus and bring the jailer and his entire household into the family of God.

4. God's Promises (15 minutes). Romans 8 reminds us that we can have confidence in God because of all He has done and continues to do in our lives in spite of our trials. Have students work in pairs to explore the selected verses of Romans 8 found on the student page. Have partners share the promises they find in the Word.

Conclude this section by saying, "When it comes to sharing or defending our faith, it would be easy to be overwhelmed with fear. But God doesn't want us to face struggles on our own. He invites us to depend on Him. He promises to help us and to always be with us."

5. No Fear (5 minutes). Provide index cards on which students can write the Bible verse of their choice. Encourage students to use the note cards in the next week to help them memorize the verse.

Closing (5 minutes). Close with silent prayer. Suggest that students confess their fears to God. Remind them of the forgiveness that is theirs through Jesus Christ.

Extending the Lesson

- Plan an activity outside of class (such as calling on church visitors, canvassing a neighborhood, or visiting a hospital or homeless shelter) to challenge teens beyond their comfort zones as well as to offer opportunities to share Jesus.
- Host an Ongoing Ambassadors for Christ weekend in your congregation.

84

Fearless Faith

1 Have You Ever?

Have you ever …

- worn a Christian T-shirt or Christian jewelry?   yes   no

- visited a hospital or nursing home?   yes   no

- talked about Jesus with a stranger?   yes   no

- talked about Jesus with a friend?   yes   no

- gone on a mission trip?   yes   no

- volunteered at a homeless shelter?   yes   no

- prayed at school?   yes   no

2 Real-Life Faith Challenges

- A sophomore is belittled for wearing a T-shirt that shows Jesus bleeding on the cross.

- A 15-year-old girl receives a low grade after refusing to write an essay on the topic "I'd sell my soul to the devil in order to …"

- Two varsity baseball players are benched for failing to attend a practice on Good Friday.

- A high school valedictorian is warned to remove any references to faith in Jesus Christ from the graduation day speech.

- Students are shot, some fatally, while meeting in a school prayer group.

3 Paul's Struggles

In the New Testament, Paul faced many struggles as he tried to share the message of Jesus Christ. Read **Acts 16:16–34**.

- What was Paul trying to do?

- What trials or struggles did he face?

- What was the outcome?

4 God's Promises

Nowhere in Scripture does God promise us trouble-free lives. In **Romans 8**, what does He promise instead?

- **Verses 1–17**

- **Verse 28**

- **Verse 31**

- **Verses 37–39**

5 No Fear

Choose one of the verses from Romans (or any other Bible verse) as your "fearless faith" reminder when you are challenged to share Jesus.

Cross Reference Chart
for Our Life in Christ® Users

Fall 2000

Study	OLIC No.	OLIC Date	OLIC Title/Bible Texts
1	1	9/3/00	God Makes the World (Genesis 1:1–2:3)
2	2	9/10/00	God Makes and Loves People (Genesis 1:26–2:25)
3	3	9/17/00	God Rescues Adam and Eve (Genesis 3:1–24)
4	4	9/24/00	God Calls Cain to Repent (Genesis 4:1–16; Romans 2:4)
5	5	10/1/00	God Saves Noah and His Family (Genesis 6:1–9:17)
6	6	10/8/00	God Calls Abram (Genesis 12:1–9)
7	7	10/15/00	God Gives Abram a Generous Heart (Genesis 13:1–18; 18:16–19:26)
8	8	10/22/00	God Keeps His Promises to Abraham (Genesis 21:1–22:19)
9	9	10/29/00	God Provides a Wife for Isaac (Genesis 24:1–67)
10	10	11/5/00	God Blesses Jacob (Genesis 25:19–34; 27:1–29)
11	11	11/12/00	God Cares for Jacob (Genesis 28:10–33:20)
12	12	11/19/00	God Protects Joseph (Genesis 37:1–36; 39:1–41:57)
13	13	11/26/00	God Helps Joseph Forgive His Brothers (Genesis 42:1–45:28; 50:15–21)

This book can be used to provide Bible studies for high school students on the same Bible story texts as the Our Life in Christ Sunday school material published by CPH. The following chart matches the studies in this book (numbers in the left column) with the corresponding lessons in the Our Life in Christ (OLIC) lessons for Fall 2000, Winter 2000–2001, and Spring 2001.

Winter 2000–2001

Study	OLIC No.	OLIC Date	OLIC Title/Bible Texts
14	1	12/3/00	God Prepares the World for Jesus (Esther 1:1–10:3; Luke 1:5–25)
15	2	12/10/00	John Prepares the Way for Jesus (Malachi 3:1–4; Philippians 1:3–11; Luke 1:57–60; 3:1–6)
16	3	12/17/00	The Savior Brings Joy (Zephaniah 3:14–18; Luke 1:39–55; Philippians 4:4–9)
17	4	12/24/00	Jesus Is Born (Luke 1:39–56; 2:1–20)
18	5	12/31/00	The Boy Jesus Visits the Temple (Luke 2:41–52; Hebrews 2:10–18; Isaiah 61:10–62:3)
19	6	1/7/01	John Tells about Jesus (Luke 3:15–17, 21–22; Matthew 11:1–19; 14:1–12)
20	7	1/14/01	Jesus Changes Water into Wine (John 2:1–11)
21	8	1/21/01	Jesus Teaches Mary and Martha (Luke 10:38–42)
22	9	1/28/01	Jesus Teaches in the Synagogue (Luke 4:14–32)
23	10	2/4/01	Jesus Helps Peter Catch Fish (Luke 5:1–11)
24	11	2/11/01	Jesus Shows His Power over Death (Mark 5:21–43; John 11:1–46; 1 Corinthians 15:12, 16–20)
25	12	2/18/01	Jesus Teaches about Love (Luke 6:27–38)
26	13	2/25/01	Jesus Is the Way to the Father (John 14:1–14; Luke 9:28–36)

Spring 2000

Study	OLIC No.	OLIC Date	OLIC Title/Bible Texts
27	1	3/4/01	Jesus Provides for Us (Matthew 14:14–21; Luke 10:25–37)
28	2	3/11/01	Jesus Gives Us the Lord's Supper (Luke 22:7–38)
29	3	3/18/01	Jesus Prays in Gethsemane (Luke 22:39–46)
30	4	3/25/01	Peter Denies Jesus (Luke 15:1–3, 11–32; 22:24–35, 54–62)
31	5	4/1/01	Pilate Condemns Jesus (Luke 22:66–23:25)
32	6	4/8/01	Jesus Is Put to Death (Luke 23:26–56; Luke 19:28–44)
33	7	4/15/01	Jesus Rises from the Dead (Luke 24:1–11; Matthew 28:1–10; 1 Corinthians 15:1–11)
34	8	4/22/01	Jesus Appears at the Sea of Galilee (John 21:1–25)
35	9	4/29/01	Saul Becomes a Christian (Acts 9:1–20)
36	10	5/6/01	Paul Begins His Ministry (Acts 9:20–31; 13:1–33)
37	11	5/13/01	Paul Preaches to Jews and Gentiles (Acts 13:44–52; 16:1–5; 2 Timothy 1:5–7; 3:14–16)
38	12	5/20/01	Paul Proclaims the Good News in Lystra, Derbe, Macedonia, and Philippi (Acts 14:8–23; 16:6–15)
39	13	5/27/01	Paul Proclaims the Good News to the Jailer at Philippi (Acts 16:16–40)